SEARCHING
FOR TRUTH

"AND YOU SHALL KNOW THE TRUTH AND
THE TRUTH SHALL MAKE YOU FREE"
JOHN 8:32

A STUDY GUIDE

JOHN MOORE

World Video Bible School®
www.wvbs.org

Searching for Truth
(A Study Guide)

Produced and published by:
World Video Bible School
25 Lantana Lane
Maxwell, TX 78656-4231
USA

Seventh printing 2015 (over 105,000 English copies in print)

Also available in the following languages:

Spanish	Korean	Swahili	Russian	Available Online

15,000 copies	5,000 copies	5,000 copies	to be printed	Apple iBookstore Amazon Kindle Google Play Nook Store

Searching for Truth books are available to read online at Google Books

Search if you will, but a book greater than the Bible will never be found. Its sixty-six books of eternal truth, authored by a perfect all-knowing God, is heaven's account of the greatest events of human history, intertwined with a proclamation of redemption, forgiveness, and hope. Its message of Christ and the cross is marvelous, and its story of love is unprecedented. Its revelation of the Lord's grace and terms of pardon is the unequivocal power of God that leads sinners to salvation (Romans 1:16). Mere mortals could never improve the wisdom it provides or the instruction it gives. The only means of improvement must therefore be in the areas of how skillfully we wield the sword of righteousness, our effectiveness in employing the teaching methods authorized in the Bible (e.g. parables), and our diligence in reaching the entire world with its truths.

In our technologically advanced era, we are blessed with many avenues for propagating God's message of hope and truth. These advancements, while serving a useful purpose in disseminating the Gospel, must not and cannot take the place of the amazing message of Christ. No matter the invention or creative delivery model, there can be no substitute for Bible truth. The problem, however, in converting souls to Jesus and to the precepts of authentic Christianity has not been the message; instead, the problem has often been in finding a way to encourage a person to interact with the sacred text. If today's church will employ the most effective means possible in reaching the lost with God's truth (as did the apostles when traveling by boat or in utilizing a courier), then a greater number of souls will be saved. This is true not because of the means of dissemination, but because the Gospel will have a greater opportunity to shine among a larger number of people. In the fall of 2004, the *video* production of *Searching for Truth* was born with this idea in mind—to produce a medium by which the Gospel could be made known to a greater number of souls (a large portion of which are typically unwilling to commit to a personal one-on-one Bible study).

The video portion of *Searching for Truth* was produced by World Video Bible School (WVBS) of Maxwell, Texas. It was completed in late 2005, and contains the following lessons: "Searching for Truth"; "Searching for Truth about the Creator"; "Searching for Truth about Authority in Religion"; "Searching for Truth about the Church"; "Searching for Truth about the House of God"; and "Searching for Truth about Baptism." I had the privilege of assisting in this project in two ways. First, I was asked to provide the basic script that eventually would be used during the filming process. Second, I was invited to be the speaker for the program. Rudy Cain, the founder of WVBS, directed and managed the project, and videographer Mathew Cain filmed, designed, and edited each video cut and graphic design. The first DVDs were released in January 2006, and in less than twelve months over *three hundred thousand* copies of *Searching for Truth* had been purchased by churches and individual Christians.

As the *Searching for Truth* DVD began to be distributed more widely, numerous requests were made that a written form of *Searching for Truth* be made available to aid viewers in their understanding, comprehension, and retention of the material presented in the video. It was also felt that the written form needed to include study questions and additional references on the various points of doctrine. It also became apparent that places existed where people needed the content of the program, but could not utilize the video (like prisons, jails, certain foreign countries, etc.). This reinforced the need for a book that not only incorporated the basic content of the program, but that also allowed a person—through use of the written material—to become his or her own teacher. In short, a study guide was needed that could be utilized in a variety of ways

and that could serve both as a companion to the video and as a "stand-alone" book for use in evangelism and edification.

The book that you now hold in your hands is a result of those needs. While it is not in every instance a word-for-word transcription of the actual text of the video, it is very close. This means that people who have access to the *Searching for Truth* DVD and who want to simultaneously use this *Study Guide* can do so while easily following the content of the video. But it also means that in some cases the book is not what I as an author would like for it to be. Verbal content is often communicated in a different style and manner than written compositions, and thus in various places you may find the material lacking in appropriate style and literary grace. For this I apologize. My original design for the written material was to serve as a script during the filming process. My prayer is that you will look beyond these limitations and my personal shortcomings as a communicator, and focus on the sublime truths of authentic Christianity and on God's message of salvation as presented in this book.

As alluded to earlier, one of our goals in producing *Searching for Truth* was to get the truth of God's word into the hands of as many people as possible so that souls everywhere might have the opportunity to live eternally with God. With the publication of the written form of *Searching for Truth*, we now can be even more effective in accomplishing that goal. [I might also mention in this regard that the text of *Searching for Truth* is now being translated into a number of foreign languages so that people who do not read or speak English will also have an opportunity to be exposed to the material. Additionally, as this book was being formatted and designed, a word-for-word transcription of the *Searching for Truth* program had just been completed, and is being used to prepare both an English version with subtitles (for those who are hearing impaired) as well as various foreign-language versions of the DVD.]

As one who is indebted to Christ, I would like to commend the material presented in this book to you—in the hope that it not only will help in your personal study of God's word, but that it also will assist you in helping others to "know the truth" (John 8:32)—the truth that sets us free.

John Moore
December 2006

AUTHOR'S NOTE: I would like to express my personal appreciation in this preface, not only to the talented and hard-working staff at World Video Bible School, but also to the many people who helped make the *Searching for Truth* video and the *Searching for Truth* book possible by donating their time and talent through interviews, post-production assistance, etc. Without their help, these works would never have been possible. May God richly bless all who have helped us in these projects and may His will always be done.

DEDICATION: This book is affectionately dedicated to Carla, my wife and best friend of more than twenty years, to our children, Jordan, Jacob, and Micah, to my parents (Grady and Janice [Combs] Moore), to Carla's parents (Carl and Janice [Sowards] Garner), and most of all to the God and Father of us all Who makes everything possible and to Whom all glory must be ascribed.

ACKNOWLEDGMENTS: The *Searching for Truth* project would not have been possible without the dedicated workers and staff of World Video Bible School, Rudy Cain, Mathew Cain, the church of Christ in Dripping Springs, Texas, and the three men who have most influenced my life and prepared me for both the ministry and the creation of *Searching for Truth*: Grady Moore, Carl Garner, and Norman Starling.

Contents

Searching for Truth

ABOUT THE TRUTH

About the Truth

ABOUT THE TRUTH

Over the years, I have conducted many funerals and have been to numerous cemeteries. And each time I conduct a funeral or visit a cemetery, I am reminded that death is certain and inevitable. Did you know that on the average, 107 people die every minute? That's 153,000 a day. That's a staggering number. It is hard to imagine *that* many people dying every day. But it happens. Death comes to the very old, the very young, and everyone in between. As much as we might *like* to go on living, all of us *will* face death.

But what happens to us when we die? Does life after death exist? If so, what *kind* of life? Does heaven exist? Does hell exist? And if so, what will happen to *you* when you die? More important, will it matter what you believed or how you lived in this life? And will the answer to those questions affect your eternal destiny?

Most people believe that the majority of those who die will end up going to heaven. But listen to what Jesus said in Matthew 7:13-14:

> Enter by the narrow gate; for wide is the gate and broad is the way that leads to destruction, and there are many who go in by it. Because narrow is the gate and difficult is the way which leads to life, and there are few who find it (Matthew 7:13-14).

Do you understand what Jesus said? There are *few* who will find life, and *many* who will choose the path to destruction. Are you among *the few* or among *the many?* Are you *certain* about *where* you will spend eternity?

What is even more sobering is what Jesus said about those who believe in Him as the Savior:

> Not everyone who says to Me, "Lord, Lord," shall enter the kingdom of heaven, but he who does the will of My Father in heaven. Many will say to Me in that day, "Lord, Lord, have we not prophesied in Your name, cast out demons in Your name, and done many wonders in Your name?" And then I will declare to them, "I never knew you; depart from Me, you who practice lawlessness!" (Matthew 7:21-23).

According to what Jesus said, there will be many *religious* people who will not enter heaven. Merely *calling* upon Jesus as our Savior is clearly not enough to prepare our souls for heaven. According to Matthew 7:21, we must *do* the will of the Father in order to go to heaven.

Now let me ask you some questions. Have *you* done the will of the Father? If you were to die today and stand before Jesus, what would He say to you? Would He say, "Depart from me, I never knew you?" Or would He welcome you into heaven? Are you absolutely *certain* about it? Have you ever questioned whether or not you were *really saved?* Do you have doubts, fears, or questions?

If you have ever had a question about life after death, then you probably have wondered about your purpose on this Earth. You may have asked questions like, "Why am I here?" and "Does God have a purpose for me?" Since time began, human beings have been asking these questions. The philosopher, the theologian, the chemist, mothers and dads, carpenters, attorneys, have all asked these questions.

Unfortunately, many false answers have been offered to those questions. Some of those answers contradict the others. It can be very confusing and distressing, especially when there seem to be so many different answers offered.

What, then, are the *true* answers to these questions? Which answers are *right?* Does it make a difference *what we believe* and *how we live* here on the Earth? Wouldn't you like to be absolutely sure? Wouldn't you like to know *the truth?*

I want you to know that none of us has to go through life wondering. The greatest Man Who ever walked the face of the Earth brought us answers to those questions—answers that can set us free from our doubts, fears, and worries. Those answers can be found in the Bible, for in that great Book Jesus tells us about truth, and about how truth can set us free.

> ...If you abide in My word, you are My disciples indeed. And you shall know the truth, and the truth shall make you free (John 8:31-32).

Those are powerful words. As we contemplate the meaning of this passage, let us notice three things about truth.

First, Jesus taught that *we can know the truth.* Truth does exist. It is real. It is not just whatever you believe it to be or what someone else believes it to be. Truth is real! There is an objective standard for determining what is right or wrong, and for what is good or evil. You do not have to wonder about whether I am telling you the truth, or whether anyone else is telling you the truth. Truth certainly exists. We *can* know what we need to do to go to heaven.

Second, not only can we *know* what is true, but *truth can set us free.* It can set us free from the bondage of sin. Jesus said, "Whoever commits sin is a slave of sin" (John 8:34). Let me ask you—Do you struggle with sin? Is it a heavy burden? Have you become a slave to money, alcohol or other drugs, pornography, etc.? What about your relationship with your spouse? Are you failing in your responsibilities as a parent? Is your life filled with resentment, jealousy, hatred, or racial prejudice? These things can weigh heavily on us. They can be great burdens on us. But I want you to know that there *is* hope, because truth can set us free from these burdens.

Not only can truth set us free from unrighteous behavior, but it also can set us free from false religious practices and the traditions of men. Like some in the first century who were being enslaved by the manmade religious traditions of the Pharisees mentioned in Matthew 23:1-33 and Mark 7:1-13, there are many people today who are burdened with various religious practices, rites, and ceremonies that are nowhere mentioned in the Bible, and that are not authorized by God. These manmade ordinances and traditions can become wearisome and burdensome. But even worse, they cause our worship to become vain. In Matthew 15:9, Jesus, in speaking about the Pharisees' traditions that were not authorized by God, said, "In vain do you worship Me, teaching as doctrines the commandments of men."

Now what about *you?* Are you in bondage to the religious traditions and ordinances of men? Have you been shackled by the teachings and commandments of men? Are you being asked to do things that God has never asked you to do? If so, I want you to know again that *there is hope,* because truth can set us free from this kind of bondage.

With knowledge of the truth, we no longer have to be held captive by uncertainty, doubt, fear, or despair. Whether it comes in the form of obvious sinful behavior, or in the form of false religious practices, sin truly captivates and enslaves. Yet Jesus and His word *can* set us free. Satan, the father of all lies and evil

practices (John 8:44), does not *have* to be our master. With truth on our side, Jesus, the Sovereign Ruler of the Universe, can be our Master and our Lord.

Third, not only can we know truth, and not only does truth set us free, but everyone needs to know that *truth is found in Jesus.* While here upon the Earth, Jesus said that He and He alone is the truth.

> *...I am the way, the truth, and the life. No one comes to the Father except through Me (John 14:6).*

If we are searching for truth, and if Jesus is *the* truth, then we should go to Jesus to find that truth. The Bible clearly teaches that truth is to be found in the person and words of Jesus. Notice again what Jesus says about truth:

> *...If you abide in My word, you are My disciples indeed. And you shall know the truth, and the truth shall make you free (John 8:31-32).*

It is the *words* of Jesus that can set us free. Truth, therefore, is a precious commodity and, in the words of one Old Testament writer, we should "buy the truth and sell it not" (Proverbs 23:23). Truth, as revealed in the Bible, is vitally important. By reading 1 Peter 1:22, we learn that truth can purify our souls. By reading 2 Thessalonians 1:7-9, we learn that we must obey the truth if we are going to avoid eternal punishment.

Life is so uncertain. The bodies of the very young, the very old, and all ages in between are in cemeteries all around the world. Some died suddenly and without warning. I wonder how many of them died *not knowing the truth.* None of us has the promise of another second upon this Earth. While some may live for 70, 80, 90, or even 100 years, one thing is for certain: as long as the Earth stands, people *are* going to die. What then? The Bible says we are going to be judged by what we have done here on Earth. According to Romans 2:2 and Romans 2:16, the standard for judgment will be the Gospel—otherwise known as the truth. All will be judged according to *truth.*

You might be thinking, "But I'm already saved. I am very sincere about what I believe, and my feelings are telling me that I've already discovered the truth." I hope you are right. I hope you *have* discovered the truth. But know one thing: sincerity alone is not enough to save you!

Before obeying the Gospel, the apostle Paul was himself very religious and very sincere about his beliefs. Yet he came to realize that he had been the chief of sinners (1 Timothy 1:15). In Acts 22, we read about the apostle Paul revealing that he had been zealous toward God, even while he had been killing Christians. Paul was *sincere,* but he was *sincerely wrong.*

Now what about *you?* Perhaps you have a great deal of zeal, but you have never really searched the Scriptures to see whether the things you believe are consistent with the Bible. Do you *know* the truth? And are you *certain* about it? If not, then join me on this journey in searching for the truth.

SECTION REVIEW: *ABOUT THE TRUTH*
Answers to the following questions can be found in the section above.

STUDY QUESTIONS

1. On average, how many people die every day? _____

2. According to Matthew 7:13-14, will there be "many" or "few" who enter the wide gate to destruction? MANY / FEW

3. According to Matthew 7:21-23:

    a. Will Jesus save all who call upon his name? YES / NO

    b. Will many religious people be lost? YES / NO

    c. What must one do to go to heaven? _____ _____ _____ _____

    _____

4. According to the verse below, is it possible to worship God in vain?   YES / NO

    And in vain they worship Me, Teaching as doctrines the commandments of men (Matthew 15:9).

5. According to John 8:31-32, Jesus said the _____ will make you free.

6. The truth can set one free from _____ _____, _____ _____

    _____, and the _____ of men.

7. According to John 14:6:

    a. Truth is to be found in _____.

    b. Can one come to the Father apart from Jesus? YES / NO

8. According to the verse below, by obeying the truth, can one purify his or her soul? YES / NO

    Since you have purified your souls in obeying the truth through the Spirit in sincere love of the brethren, love one another fervently with a pure heart (1 Peter 1:22).

9. According to the verse below, will those who do NOT obey the truth be punished eternally? YES / NO

    And to give you who are troubled rest with us when the Lord Jesus is revealed from heaven with His mighty angels, in flaming fire taking vengeance on those who do not know God, and on those who do not obey the gospel of our Lord Jesus Christ. These shall be punished with everlasting destruction from the presence of the Lord and from the glory of His power (2 Thessalonians 1:7-9).

10. According to the verses below, on the day of judgment, every soul will be judged according to the _____ (the Gospel).

    But we know that the judgment of God is according to truth against those who practice such things (Romans 2:2).

    In the day when God will judge the secrets of men by Jesus Christ, according to my gospel (Romans 2:16).

11. Before the apostle Paul became a Christian, he was sincere in his religious beliefs, but he was sincerely _____.

12. Can sincerity alone save a soul from hell? YES / NO

An ANSWER KEY for the STUDY QUESTIONS is provided in the back of the book.

DECISION POINTS

A. If at some point in your study of *Searching For Truth* you discover that what you have sincerely believed or practiced is inconsistent with the Bible's teaching, will you change to comply with the will of God? YES / NO

B. According to Matthew 7:21-23, have you done the will of the Father? YES / NO

Searching for Truth

ABOUT THE CREATOR

As we observe the Universe, the Earth, and the amazing human body, it is easy to conclude that these things could not have occurred by accident. They are, in fact, the product of an intelligent Creator. But what kind of Creator? What do we really know about Him? Does He really care about His creation? What is He like? Can we know Him? And where can we go to find the answers to such questions?

INTRODUCTION

Life is a search for answers. *True* answers regarding our eternal destiny are the ones we value the most. In searching for these answers, it seems that perhaps the best place to begin such a journey would be to examine our home—planet Earth—where God's creation is so highly visible. I really enjoy walking in the forest or traveling in the country—away from the crowded highways and marketplaces. Being there reminds me of the powerful hand of God. But is this where we encounter God? Is nature where we come to find God? In our search for truth, let us ask three important questions.

1. **What can nature tell us about God?**
2. **How do we know the mind of God?**
3. **What does the Bible tell us about God?**

Let's examine each of these questions in turn.

WHAT CAN NATURE TELL US ABOUT GOD?

Over the centuries, numerous philosophers, scientists, and theologians have acknowledged the existence of a God. Their acknowledgment, in part, was based on the evidence of God in nature. William Paley, a theologian of the eighteenth century, became well known for his argument concerning the existence of God based on nature.

The works of nature want only to be contemplated. When contemplated, they have everything within them which can astonish by their greatness; for, of the vast scale of operation, through which our discoveries carry us, we see an intelligent Power. Every organized natural body, in the provisions which it contains for its sustentation and propagations, testifies a care on the part of the Creator. We are on all sides surrounded by such bodies; examined in their parts, wonderfully curious; compared with one another, no less wonderfully diversified. There is no subject of which, in its full extent, the latitude is so great, as that of natural history applied to the proof of an intelligent Creator (*Natural Theology*).

It is true: God *has* revealed Himself in nature—a fact that the Bible clearly substantiates as well. Read what the apostle Paul wrote as he acknowledged the evidence of God in nature.

For since the creation of the world His invisible attributes are clearly seen, being understood by the things that are made, even His eternal power and Godhead, so that they are without excuse (Romans 1:20).

From this verse, we learn that mankind has no excuse for *not* believing in God. God has clearly revealed Himself in the world. As we examine the world, the Universe, and even our own bodies, we can come to see that this is all evidence of a Creator. But let's see what a scientist has to say about this:

You can't have a poem without a poet, or a house without a house builder. You can't have design without an intelligent Designer. The complexity within a cell, the complexity of Earth's atmospheric conditions, the distances between the planets—everything was put here for a purpose. If we look at the human nervous system, for example, we see that it is composed of billions of cells, and that it was purposely arranged to be able to conduct a nerve signal from one part of the body to the other. On a microscopic level, we see that a single cell has ion-gated channels, voltage-gated channels, and a membrane potential. It was specifically designed to do one thing—carry a nerve impulse from one cell to another. When you look deep inside the cell, you find the DNA—the biological code of life that allows the cell to perpetuate itself. Within the cell, you have an incredibly complex biochemical code, and yet we are expected to believe that it "just happened by chance"? Over and over again, as you look throughout nature, you see what is almost like a "neon arrow" pointing to a Creator, an intelligent Designer. That designer is God.

Brad Harrub, Ph.D.
Neurobiologist

God, it would seem, is practically screaming to us through the world around us, saying, "*I am here, I exist!*" But what does the world around us reveal about Him? It tells us that He is an intelligent, masterful Architect Who is capable of creating and sustaining this complex Universe. It tells us that He is a Creator of amazing organisms and intricately designed systems. It tells us that He is much greater, and more powerful, than any force we could ever imagine.

However, as impressed as we may be by this marvelous creation, we cannot know the mind of God by observing a tree—or nature in *any* form. I cannot know whether God loves me. I cannot know whether there is a heaven or hell. I cannot know what to do to be saved by simply looking at the ground beneath my feet. How, then, do I know the mind of God? How can I know His will for me? And how can I know what I must do to be saved?

SECTION REVIEW: *WHAT CAN NATURE TELL US ABOUT GOD?*

Answers to the following questions can be found in the section above.

STUDY QUESTIONS

1. William Paley's argument for the existence of God is based on the evidence of God found in _____.

2. According to Romans 1:20, people who refuse to believe in God are without _____, because God has provided so much evidence of His existence.

3. If there is design in something, then there must be an _____ _____.

4. The evidence around us in nature tells us that God is an intelligent, _____ _____ Who is capable of creating and sustaining this complex Universe.

5. Humans cannot know the mind of God by observing a _____—or _____ in *any* form.

6. By observing the evidence of God in nature, can we know God's will for our lives? YES / NO

7. By observing nature, can we know whether heaven or hell exists? YES / NO

8. Can a person know what to do to become saved by examining the grass, rocks, trees, etc.? YES / NO

An ANSWER KEY for the STUDY QUESTIONS is provided in the back of the book.

DECISION POINTS

A. According to the verse below, must you believe in God to be saved? YES / NO

> *But without faith* it is *impossible to please* Him, *for he who comes to God must believe* that *He is, and that He is a rewarder of those who diligently seek Him (Hebrews 11:6).*

B. Do you believe in God? YES / NO

TALKING POINTS

A. How do things like the complexity of the cell, or the complexity of the Universe, provide evidence of God?

B. Why can humans *not* understand all they need to know about God by merely looking at things around them in nature?

HOW DO WE KNOW THE MIND OF GOD?

In the Bible, the apostle Paul addressed that very topic.

For what man knows the things of a man except the spirit of the man which is in him? Even so, no one knows the things of God except the Spirit of God. Now we have received, not the spirit of the world, but the Spirit who is from God, that we might know the things that have been freely given to us by God. These things we also speak, not in words which man's wisdom teaches, but which the Holy Spirit teaches... (1 Corinthians 2:11-13).

From this passage we learn that man, on his own, has no way of knowing the mind of God. In other words, we cannot know God's mind just by looking at the natural world or by searching within ourselves.

Second, we learn that God made known His mind by means of His Spirit. The Spirit revealed to man what man, on his own, never could have known.

Third, we learn that the revelation of God's mind is made possible by the Spirit's teaching. We come to know the mind of God, not through a feeling that we have in our heart, but through what the Spirit teaches in words. Those words are found in the Bible. The Bible is the mind of God made known by the Spirit of God. It is referred to as "Scripture." Let's look at what the Bible says about the origin and purpose of Scripture.

All Scripture is given by inspiration of God, and is profitable for doctrine, for reproof, for correction, for instruction in righteousness, that the man of God may be complete, thoroughly equipped for every good work (2 Timothy 3:16-17).

The Scriptures, Paul says, came by inspiration. In that passage, the word "inspiration" literally means "God breathed."

When you go back to the Greek, in which the New Testament was originally written, you find that the word is *theopneustos*, which is a combined word. The first part means "God," while the second part means "breathed." So Paul is saying that all Scripture is actually "breathed by God."

Chuck Horner
Bible Instructor and Minister

In other words, as God breathed into man and he became a living soul, God breathed into the message we call "the Bible" a life. The Bible is living and active. We do not have a dead letter. We have a living message that came directly from the mind of God.

Keith Mosher Sr.
Bible Instructor and Minister

Knowing this first, that no prophecy of Scripture is of any private interpretation, for prophecy never came by the will of man, but holy men of God spoke as they were moved by the Holy Spirit (2 Peter 1:20-21).

Thus, we can clearly see that the Bible is not the product of man. The Bible is the product of the Holy Spirit. It is the mind of God. Thus, we can go to the Bible to learn the truth about God. Let us answer, then, the third major question: "What does the Bible tell us about God?"

SECTION REVIEW: *HOW CAN WE KNOW THE MIND OF GOD?*

Answers to the following questions can be found in the section above.

STUDY QUESTIONS

1. Apart from the Bible, can man know the mind of God? YES / NO

2. Can a person know the mind of God through a simple "feeling" in the heart? YES / NO

3. The Bible reveals the mind of God and is made known by the Spirit of God. The Bible is also referred to as _____.

4. According to 2 Timothy 3:16-17, is all scripture given by the inspiration of God? YES / NO

5. It is only in the _____ that we can come to know the mind of God.

6. The English word "inspiration" comes from two Greek words that mean _____ _____.

7. The Bible is the product of the _____ _____.

8. Does 2 Peter 1:20-21 teach that scripture (the Bible) is the result of man's own mind? YES / NO

An ANSWER KEY for the STUDY QUESTIONS is provided in the back of the book.

DECISION POINTS

A. Do you believe that the Bible is God's inspired word? YES / NO

B. Are you truly seeking to understand the word of God? YES / NO

TALKING POINTS

A. Discuss various characteristics of the Bible which prove that it could *not* be the product of men's minds.

B. Why did God need to provide man with His words and thoughts in a *written* form?

WHAT DOES THE BIBLE TELL US ABOUT GOD?

To answer this question, let's examine a speech made by the apostle Paul at a place called Mars Hill, which is located in Athens, Greece. That speech is found in the seventeenth chapter of the book of Acts. As we begin, let's put that speech in its historical context.

After Paul was converted to Christ, it was not long before he began spreading the Gospel ("good news") of Christ. As he traveled to cities such as Lystra, Philippi, and Thessalonica, he would spend his time telling others about Jesus and the kingdom of God.

However, when he came to Athens, he encountered a city that was completely immersed in idolatry. The people of Athens were ex-tremely religious—so religious and superstitious that they even erected an altar with an inscription that read: "TO THE UN-KNOWN GOD." Perhaps they feared the possibility of offending some deity unknown to them, so they erected this altar in honor of this God of Whom they knew nothing.

Paul also encountered various philosophers and the educated elite of his day. Athens was well known for its philosophers, as well as for its emphasis on politics, literature, and learning. And yet, as Paul stood on Mars Hill (where religious and moral court proceedings often were conducted), he expressed that the true Creator of the Universe was *very much* interested in, and involved with, the affairs of men. Let's now read what Paul revealed to the people of Athens about the God Whom they referred to as "the unknown God."

> ...*Men of Athens, I perceive that in all things you are very religious; for as I was passing through and considering the objects of your worship, I even found an altar with this inscription: TO THE UNKNOWN GOD. Therefore, the One whom you worship without knowing, Him I proclaim to you: God, who made the world and everything in it, since He is Lord of heaven and earth, does not dwell in temples made with hands. Nor is He worshiped with men's hands, as though He needed anything, since He gives to all life, breath, and all things. And He has made from one blood every nation of men to dwell on all the face of the earth, and has determined their preappointed times and the boundaries of their dwellings (Acts 17:22-26).*

As we attempt to answer the question, "What does the Bible tell us about God?," we learn three things from Paul's speech.

1.   God is the Creator of all things.

God made the world and *everything* in it. To suggest that this beautiful creation and this highly complex Universe are the products of mere happenstance is unthinkable. In Paul's day, the belief that God existed was a well-known and well-established belief. Yet, as Paul pointed out, there is *only one God* Who has created everything. However, as Paul would argue later in his speech, we must not worship God ignorantly. We must not be like those people of Athens who worshiped God in a vain manner, according to the dictates of their own conscience. Paul had revealed to them that God is the sovereign Ruler of the Universe, and that He is the Creator of all things. Since He *is* the Creator of all things, we must worship Him according to the dictates of His will. We must not worship God ignorantly.

2.   God is within the reach of all.

Let us also notice from the text of Acts 17 that God is within the reach of all. Read what Paul said as he continued with his speech.

> *And He has made from one blood every nation of men to dwell on all the face of the earth, and has determined their preappointed times and the boundaries of their dwellings, so that they should seek the Lord, in the hope that they might grope for Him and find Him, though He is not far from each one of us; for in Him we live and move and have our being, as also some of your own poets have said, "For we are also His offspring." There-*

> *fore, since we are the offspring of God, we ought not to think that the Divine Nature is like gold or silver or stone, something shaped by art and man's devising (Acts 17:26-29).*

Those words from the apostle Paul are very comforting because they reveal to us that God is involved in His creation. He has set the bounds of man's habitation, and He has been involved in the affairs of men and with the rise and fall of nations. Even now, the bad things that happen to us in this life can serve a useful purpose—to remind us to seek after God.

When we find God, we realize that He is not like the gods of paganism. He is very different from those gods. The one true and living God is not made of stones or gold, and is not fashioned by man's devices. He does not dwell in temples made by human hands. The one true and living God is spirit. He possesses personality. The one true, living God is concerned with the affairs of men.

> He is One Who cares for us. He provides for us. He provides for our needs, both physically and spiritually. He sends the rain on the just and the unjust. He sent His Son to die for all who were unjust, that we might become His children. Having the ability to go to live with Him forever in His house is beyond our ability to comprehend. The term "Father" conjures up in our minds the idea of a loving family.
>
> B. J. Clarke
> Minister

In 1 John 4:8, the apostle John said that "God is love." Not only is He love, but according to the Bible He also is our Father. He is our heavenly Father. As a Father, He longs to have a relationship with those He has created. Indeed, God wants us to love Him. We desire to be loved as well. Each one of us desires to belong. Each one of us desires a relationship. The God of the Bible can provide that.

> Man, throughout the ages, has "sought to belong." When the people built the Tower of Babel, they sought to make a name for themselves, and had joined together for immoral purposes. In other ages throughout history, people sought the love that was missing in their lives. They gave up on the good things that were right before them. They had proper relationships with their friends and families, yet they sought other things that were not right. The mental-health profession today is replete with resources for people to use as they seek out this "missing love" in their lives. People go to counselors, psychologists, and psychiatrists day in and day out. They follow them around the country, seeking an ever-elusive answer. Yet the answer they seek is actually right in front of them. God has provided love for mankind. He has provided an opportunity for us to grow and become stronger, yet we sometimes ignore it. What we need to do is to recognize that

God gave His only begotten Son that we might live. Although we can gain help from other sources, what we really need to do is to go back to the Bible. We need to study it, because it explains the great love that God has given us. There is no need to seek further, for the answers are right before us.

Dr. Stephen Springer
Licensed Professional Counselor and University Professor

Yes, God truly does love us. He cares deeply about us. He is fully aware of our sorrows and our heartaches. He is within the reach of each and every one of us. As the apostle Paul said, it is in Him that we live, move, and have our very existence. In other words, it is in God that we find purpose in our existence.

Let us consider not only that God is the Creator of all, and that He is within the reach of every one of us, but also that God wants to give salvation to everyone.

3. God gives salvation to all.

Truly, these times of ignorance God overlooked, but now commands all men everywhere to repent, because He has appointed a day on which He will judge the world in righteousness by the Man whom He has ordained. He has given assurance of this to all by raising Him from the dead (Acts 17:30-31).

God will one day judge the world. Because He will one day judge the world, He has made a way for everyone to be saved. Indeed, *God wants everyone to be saved.* Thus, He has given all of us equal opportunity to be saved by means of the resurrection of His Son, Jesus.

One thing that we need to understand is that God loves all sinners—everywhere, in every place, regardless of what they have done. Neither the magnitude nor the multitude of our sins is a barrier to our salvation. Even the "chief of sinners" (as the apostle Paul described himself) received the grace of God. In 1 Corinthians 15:10, he said, "By the grace of God I am what I am." Paul had done much damage to the church, yet Jesus gave him forgiveness.

B. J. Clarke
Minister

The Lord will forgive anyone who truly turns to Him. We read in 2 Peter 3:9, "The Lord is not slack concerning His promise, as some count slackness, but is longsuffering toward us, not willing that any should perish but that all should come to repentance."

Garland Elkins
Bible Instructor and Minister

God is not willing that *anyone* should perish. He wants *everyone* to come to repentance. According to John 3:16, God loved the world so much that He gave His only begotten Son to die so that you and I do not have to suffer eternal punishment. God wants everyone to be saved.

While God wants to save everyone, God expects something in return.

Truly, these times of ignorance God overlooked, but now commands all men everywhere to repent (Acts 17:30).

Do you see what God expects? According to the apostle Paul, God wants all of us to repent. Read what Jesus said about this in the Gospel according to Luke:

I tell you, no; but unless you repent you will all likewise perish (Luke 13:3).

The bottom line is that repentance is a change of heart and mind. When one repents by changing his heart and mind about sin, and turns to do what is commanded by God, that person has come to repentance.

Alfred Washington
Minister

Repentance is a mental decision that says, "God told me to do this, and if I don't do it, I'm sinning against God. God sent His Son for me. He loves me. I know I'm hurting Him if I don't repent. So, I'm going to change the way I'm thinking and I'm going to do whatever God tells me to do." That is why repentance is such a tough command. A person has to say, "I'm not going my own way anymore. I'm going to do what God told me to do." Repentance is a change of mind based on godly sorrow.

Keith Mosher Sr.
Bible Instructor and Minister

Repentance is expected of all men. It does not matter whether they are rich or poor, educated or uneducated. It does not matter where a person is born. It does not matter who our parents were, or what our children may one day become. God expects *everyone* to repent.

But *why* is repentance necessary? Why does God call upon you and me to repent?

Because He has appointed a day on which He will judge the world in righteousness... (Acts 17:31).

For we must all appear before the judgment seat of Christ, that each one may receive the things done *in the body, according to what he has done, whether good or bad. Knowing, therefore, the terror of the Lord, we persuade men... (2 Corinthians 5:10-11).*

Repentance, then, is necessary because God will one day judge the world. Each one of us will be held accountable for what we have done, as well as what we have failed to do. God expects us to repent. He expects us to turn from false ways and ideas. And if we do not, we *will* suffer under the judgment of God. We *will* suffer His wrath and terror.

You might be asking: "If God wants to save everyone, why would He punish those who do not repent?" The answer is because God is *just* (Revelation 15:3) and *righteous* (Romans 2:5). Because He is *just,* He must punish wrongdoing. Because He is *righteous,* He must discipline those who are rebellious. Imagine, for example, a judge in your own community who refused to punish convicted criminals. Would you consider this judge to be just or righteous? Would you not expect (and, in fact, demand!) that a judge punish those who did not abide by the law? In a similar way, God, the Judge of all the Earth (Genesis 18:25), will punish those who do not abide by *His* law. God, as a just God, does want everyone to be saved. But He also will punish those who do not repent. Consider the judgment, as described by the apostle John.

And I saw the dead, small and great, standing before God, and the books were opened. And another book was opened,

which is the Book *of Life. And the dead were judged according to their works, by the things which were written in the books. (Revelation 20:12).*

We all are going to stand before the judgment seat of God. Romans 14:11-12 and 2 Corinthians 5:10 both state that we will be judged "according to our works." This makes the judgment *very* serious.

Curtis Cates
Bible Instructor and Minister

All of us will be at the judgment. That includes *you.* One day you will stand before God and give an account for the things you have done here on the Earth. If you repent and turn to God, you can be saved and live eternally. We can be saved by the power of God and the resurrection of Jesus Christ from the dead.

In our search for truth, let us consider the three things we have learned:

1. **We cannot know the mind of God by observing the creation.** While the creation around us certainly provides ample evidence that God exists, we cannot know His mind by merely observing that creation.

2. **God has revealed Himself to us through the Holy Spirit.** God has made known His mind by means of the written word—the Bible.

3. **The Bible tells us that God is the Creator of all, that He is within the reach of all, and that He wants to save everyone.**

SECTION REVIEW: *WHAT DOES THE BIBLE TELL US ABOUT GOD?*

Answers to the following questions can be found in the section above.

STUDY QUESTIONS

1. The word "Gospel" means _____ _____.

2. According to Acts 17:22-26, is God the Lord of Heaven and Earth? YES / NO

3. According to Acts 17:24, Does the one true living God dwell in temples made with hands? YES / NO

4. According to Acts 17:30-31, everyone must _____.

5. According to Acts 17:27, God is not _____ from any one of us.

6. According to the verse below, the apostle John said that "God is _____."

    He who does not love does not know God, for God is love (1 John 4:8).

7. Jesus said in Luke 13:3 that unless people _____, they will perish.

8. According to the verse below, does God love you? YES / NO

    For God so loved the world that He gave His only begotten Son, that whoever believes in Him should not perish but have everlasting life (John 3:16).

9. Does the Lord want you to perish? YES / NO

10. Does the verse below say that God is a *just* God? YES / NO

    They sing the song of Moses, the servant of God, and the song of the Lamb, saying: "Great and marvelous are *Your works, Lord God Almighty! Just and true* are *Your ways, O King of the saints!" (Revelation 15:3)*

11. Would an earthly judge be just if he or she refused to punish convicted criminals? YES / NO

12. According to Revelation 20:12, all people will one day be judged according to their works. Does that include you? YES / NO

An ANSWER KEY for the STUDY QUESTIONS is provided in the back of the book.

DECISION POINTS

A. Have you ever worshiped God in vain or ignorantly? YES / NO

B. If at some point in this study you discover that you are worshiping God in vain, will you repent? YES / NO

C. Are you ready at this moment to stand before God to give account of your deeds? YES / NO

TALKING POINTS

A. Why must God punish people who are sinful and who have not repented of their sins?

B. According to 2 Peter 3:9, God is "longsuffering." What does that mean?

CONCLUSION

God wants to save you. The great Creator of this Universe loves you and wants you to respond to His will.

Will you respond to His will? In Paul's day, some rejected the truth about the Creator. They did not repent of their sins, once they were confronted with what is right.

But what about *you?* What if, in our search for truth, you discover that what you have been taught, or what you now believe, is inconsistent with what the Bible teaches? Will you turn? Will you change? Will you do things God's way? In our journey—our search for truth—I hope you will examine yourself to see whether or not you are truly in the faith. Jesus said, "You shall know the truth, and the truth shall make you free" (John 8:32).

CHAPTER REVIEW
Answers to the following questions can be found within this chapter.

STUDY QUESTIONS

1. According to Romans 1:20, is God's existence clearly seen in the world? YES / NO

2. According to 2 Peter 1:20-21, did scripture originate with God or man? _____

3. According to 2 Corinthians 5:10, everyone will stand before the _____ seat of Christ.

4. According to John 3:16 and 2 Peter 3:9, does God want everyone to be saved? YES / NO

FOCUS QUESTIONS

1. Is the Bible a product of *just* the minds of humans? YES / NO

2. Can people know God's will for their lives merely by what they feel in their hearts? YES / NO

3. Will God punish those who do not abide by His law? YES / NO

An ANSWER KEY for the STUDY QUESTIONS and FOCUS QUESTIONS is provided in the back of the book.

THINGS YOU SHOULD KNOW

- God is the Creator of all.
- Man cannot know the mind of God by observing the creation around him.
- Man, by himself, cannot know the mind of God.
- The Spirit of God made known the mind of God through teaching.
- God is within the reach of all.
- God offers salvation to all.
- God will punish those who do not repent.

DIGGING DEEPER...

The material below is intended for those people who would like to study this subject further. It contains information that was not necessarily discussed in the lesson.

 ### GOD IS THE CREATOR

In the beginning God created the heavens and the earth (Genesis 1:1).

When I consider Your heavens, the work of Your fingers, The moon and the stars, which You have ordained, What is man that You are mindful of him, And the son of man that You visit him? (Psalm 8:3-4).

The heavens declare the glory of God; And the firmament shows His handiwork (Psalm 19:1).

Know that the LORD, He is God; It is He who has made us, and not we ourselves; We are His people and the sheep of His pasture (Psalm 100:3).

God, who made the world and everything in it, since He is Lord of heaven and earth, does not dwell in temples made with hands (Acts 17:24).

You are worthy, O Lord, To receive glory and honor and power; For You created all things, And by Your will they exist and were created (Revelation 4:11).

THINGS TO THINK ABOUT...WHEN DIGGING DEEPER

1. Does Genesis 1:1 teach that God created the heavens and the earth? YES / NO

2. Do Psalm 8:3-4 and 19:1 teach that God made the heavens and all they contain? YES / NO

3. According to Psalm 100:3, Who made us? _____

4. God "made the _____ and _____ in it" (Acts 17:24).

5. According to Revelation 4:11, God created _____

_____.

GOD IS OMNISCIENT (ALL KNOWING)

For the ways of man are *before the eyes of the LORD, And He ponders all his paths (Proverbs 5:21).*

The eyes of the LORD are *in every place, Keeping watch on the evil and the good (Proverbs 15:3).*

Remember the former things of old, For I am *God, and* there is *no other; I* am *God, and* there is *none like Me, Declaring the end from the beginning, And from ancient times* things *that are not* yet *done, Saying, "My counsel shall stand, And I will do all My pleasure" (Isaiah 46:9-10).*

And He said to them, "You are those who justify yourselves before men, but God knows your hearts. For what is highly esteemed among men is an abomination in the sight of God" (Luke 16:15).

And they prayed and said, "You, O Lord, who know the hearts of all, show which of these two You have chosen" (Acts 1:24).

And there is no creature hidden from His sight, but all things are *naked and open to the eyes of Him to whom we* must give *account (Hebrews 4:13).*

THINGS TO THINK ABOUT...WHEN DIGGING DEEPER

6. Do Proverbs 5:21 and 15:3 teach that God knows *everything* humans do? YES / NO

7. According to Isaiah 46:9-10, does God know what will happen even before it occurs? YES / NO

8. God knows each person's _____ (Luke 16:15 and Acts 1:24).

9. According to Hebrews 4:13, _____ _____ are naked and open to the eyes of God.

10. According to Hebrews 4:13, we have to give _____ to God for our actions.

GOD IS OMNIPOTENT (ALL POWERFUL)

I know that You can do everything, And that no purpose of Yours can be withheld from You (Job 42:2).

By the word of the LORD the heavens were made, And all the host of them by the breath of His mouth. He gathers the waters of the sea together as a heap; He lays up the deep in storehouses. Let all the earth fear the LORD; Let all the inhabitants of the world stand in awe of Him. For He spoke, and it was done; *He commanded, and it stood fast (Psalm 33:6-9).*

But Jesus looked at them and said, "With men it is *impossible, but not with God; for with God all things are possible" (Mark 10:27).*

By faith we understand that the worlds were framed by the word of God, so that the things which are seen were not made of things which are visible (Hebrews 11:3).

"I am the Alpha and the Omega, the Beginning and the End," says the Lord, "who is and who was and who is to come, the Almighty" (Revelation 1:8).

THINGS TO THINK ABOUT...WHEN DIGGING DEEPER

11. Job states that God can do _____ (Job 42:2).

12. God is so powerful that "He _____, and it was done; He _____, and it stood fast" (Psalm 33:6-9).

13. "For with God _____ _____ are possible" (Mark 10:27).

14. According to Hebrews 11:3, did God make the worlds by using material that already existed. YES / NO

15. According to Revelation 1:8, the Lord is _____.

GOD IS OMNIPRESENT (EVERYWHERE)

But will God indeed dwell on the earth? Behold, heaven and the heaven of heavens cannot contain You. How much less this temple which I have built! (1 Kings 8:27).

Where can I go from Your Spirit? Or where can I flee from Your presence? If I ascend into heaven, You are *there; If I make my bed in hell, behold, You are there. If I take the wings of the morning, And dwell in the uttermost parts of the sea, Even there Your hand shall lead me, And Your right hand shall hold me (Psalm 139:7-10).*

Ask, and it will be given to you; seek, and you will find; knock, and it will be opened to you. For everyone who asks receives, and he who seeks finds, and to him who knocks it will be opened (Matthew 7:7-8).

So that they should seek the Lord, in the hope that they might grope for Him and find Him, though He is not far from each one of us (Acts 17:27).

Who shall separate us from the love of Christ? Shall tribulation, or distress, or persecution, or famine, or nakedness, or peril, or sword? As it is written: "For Your sake we are killed all day long; We are accounted as sheep for the slaughter." Yet in all these things we are more than conquerors through Him who loved us. For I am persuaded that neither death nor life, nor angels nor principalities nor powers, nor things present nor things to come, nor height nor depth, nor any other created thing, shall be able to separate us from the love of God which is in Christ Jesus our Lord (Romans 8:35-39).

THINGS TO THINK ABOUT...WHEN DIGGING DEEPER

16. Solomon's statement in 1 Kings 8:27 shows us that God is everywhere because heaven and the heaven of heavens

    _____ _____ God.

17. Psalm 139:7 teaches there is no where we can _____ from God's presence.

18. Do Matthew 7:7-8 and Acts 17:27 teach that when we search for God, will we be able to find Him? YES / NO

19. According to Acts 17:27, is God close to some people and far away from others? YES / NO

20. Does Romans 8:35-39 teach that some things can separate us from God's love? YES / NO

GOD IS OMNIBENEVOLENT (ALL KIND)

Through the LORD's mercies we are not consumed, Because His compassions fail not. They are new every morning; Great is Your faithfulness (Lamentations 3:22-23).

Therefore do not worry, saying, "What shall we eat?" or "What shall we drink?" or "What shall we wear?" For after all these

things the Gentiles seek. For your heavenly Father knows that you need all these things. But seek first the kingdom of God and His righteousness, and all these things shall be added to you (Matthew 6:31-33).

For this is good and acceptable in the sight of God our Savior, who desires all men to be saved and to come to the knowledge of the truth (1 Timothy 2:3-4).

Every good gift and every perfect gift is from above, and comes down from the Father of lights, with whom there is no variation or shadow of turning (James 1:17).

The Lord is not slack concerning His promise, as some count slackness, but is longsuffering toward us, not willing that any should perish but that all should come to repentance (2 Peter 3:9).

He who does not love does not know God, for God is love (1 John 4:8).

THINGS TO THINK ABOUT...WHEN DIGGING DEEPER

21. "His _____ fail not. They are new every morning" (Lamentations 3:22-23).

22. Does Matthew 6:31-33 teach God will provide our physical needs if we are righteous and seek Him? YES / NO

23. According to James 1:17, every _____

    _____ and every _____ _____ comes from God.

24. According to 1 Timothy 2:3-4 and 2 Peter 3:9, does God want everyone to be saved? YES / NO

25. "God is _____" (1 John 4:8).

An ANSWER KEY for the DIGGING DEEPER QUESTIONS is provided in the back of the book.

ABOUT AUTHORITY IN RELIGION

In today's religious world, there is a great deal of debate about what is right and what is wrong. When it comes to matters of faith, there are a number of differing viewpoints. But which one is correct? And who determines what is right? Who gets to make the rules? Who or what is the final authority in religious matters? Is it the church, the Bible, a creed book, or a council of scholars? Who, or what, has authority in religious matters? In other words, who makes the rules? And where can we go to find the answers?

INTRODUCTION

Knowing what the rules are, and where to find them, are two things that are absolutely essential for almost any endeavor. On the field of athletic competition, an established rulebook and an established authority are a "must." When teams meet to compete in the athletic arena, they do so, having agreed upon an established rulebook that has been authored and approved beforehand by an authoritative person or board. The principle of having an established set of rules or a set authority is a widely accepted principle, whether it has to do with sports, a civic organization, a school activity, a church, or a nation. Everyone understands the importance and necessity of having a recognized authority or an established rulebook.

In every sporting event, there must be a recognized authority and an established set of rules. Without a rulebook or an authoritative board or person, the games could never be played. Take, for example, the summer Olympic Games that are held every four years at various locations around the world. Those countries and their participants can, in a uniform and unified way, participate in those games because they have all agreed upon the necessity of there being one standard authority and one set of rules to be followed. For the Olympic Games, that standard authority is organized with the supreme authority at the top, known as the International Olympic Committee. The Committee's job is to appoint from among its members a president and an executive board. The president and the executive board then enact codes and guidelines, and appoint a director general to provide assistance with the writing and the implementation of those rules. Out of this process, a rulebook is established. This rulebook then becomes the authoritative document for determining the boundaries, the rules of each game, and how those games will be judged. Without a chain of authority and a rulebook, the summer Olympic Games could never be played. Without a rulebook, there would be confusion and chaos. An agreed-upon standard of authority and a rulebook are an absolute "must."

Charles Smith
Referee

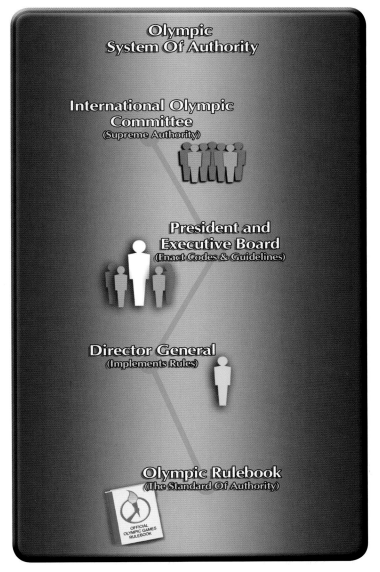

Now, let us turn our attention to something far more important than any sporting event. Let's turn our attention to the realm of religion, and ask: "Is there a single authority in religion? Is there a single, authoritative document or rulebook in religion?"

If—in determining the rules for the church, how it is to be organized, or how it is to worship—one person consults a creed book to find the guidelines, another person consults a decision made by a convention of delegates, and still another group makes a decision based on what they "feel in their hearts," these individuals will be unable to come to *any* kind of suitable agreement. They will be unable to play on the same "field," and there will be certain division and disunity.

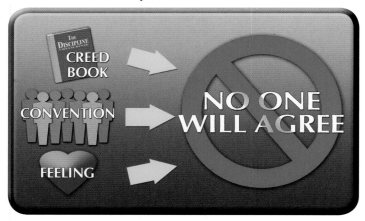

If unity and agreement are to occur—and the absolute truth about what to believe, how to live, and how to worship is to ever be realized—then we must begin by determining who has the right to make the rules and where those rules are written down. Knowing what our standard of authority is will affect our eternal destiny! The search for truth about authority in religion, then, is quite crucial. Therefore, let us ask four important questions:

1. **What is authority?**
2. **Who or what is the authority in religion?**
3. **How is this authority made known?**
4. **Is there more than one standard of authority today?**

WHAT IS AUTHORITY?

Let us begin our search by asking: "What is authority?" We have used the word "authority" several times up to this point, but what exactly does it mean? According to the *Oxford English Dictionary,* the word "authority" means "the right or power to enforce obedience; moral or legal supremacy; the right to command or give an ultimate decision."

A good example of this definition is found in Matthew 8:9, where a Roman centurion (who had asked Jesus to heal his servant) said:

> *For I also am a man under authority, having soldiers under me. And I say to this* one, *"Go," and he goes; and to another, "Come," and he comes; and to my servant, "Do this," and he does* it *(Matthew 8:9).*

Authority, then, involves the right to command and the power to make laws. The root word of authority is the word "author." An author is "the person who originates or gives existence to anything" *(Oxford English Dictionary).* The word refers to the person who is the founder or inventor of something. Thus the word "authority" conveys one or more of the following ideas:

- The right or power to command or give ultimate decisions
- Moral or legal supremacy
- The originator or founder of something

But what about religious authority? As we continue our search for truth regarding authority in religion, let's ask our second major question: "Who or what is the authority in religion?"

SECTION REVIEW: *WHAT IS AUTHORITY?*
Answers to the following questions can be found in the section above.

STUDY QUESTIONS

1. In almost every area of life, it is important to know what the rules are and _____ _____

   _____ _____ .

2. Is it important to have a standard, recognized rulebook (or authority) in games, sports, civic clubs, school organizations, nations, and the church? YES / NO

3. According to the *Oxford English Dictionary,* the word "authority" means "the right or power to enforce obedience; moral or legal supremacy; the

   right to _____ or give an ultimate _____."

4. Does religious division exist among those who profess to follow Christ? YES / NO

5. According to the verse below, does God want there to be division among His followers? YES / NO

   Now I plead with you, brethren, by the name of our Lord Jesus Christ, that you all speak the same thing, and that there be no divisions among you, but that you be perfectly joined together in the same mind and in the same judgment (1 Corinthians 1:10).

6. If unity and agreement are to occur among the followers of Christ, must those followers agree upon a single standard of authority (i.e. agree upon a single rulebook)? YES / NO

An ANSWER KEY for the STUDY QUESTIONS is provided in the back of the book.

DECISION POINTS

A. Are you willing to abide by God's instructions that His people "all speak the same thing" so that there will be no divisions in the Lord's church (1 Corinthians 1:10)? YES / NO

B. Are you willing to submit to God and His word, the Bible, as the ultimate Authority in your life? YES / NO

TALKING POINTS

A. Why do players, coaches, and teams not have the right to change, delete from, or add to the rulebook?

B. In determining the rules for the church and its organization, what will happen if one group turns to a creed book to find the guidelines, another group appeals to what a convention of delegates has decided, and still another group makes a subjective decision based on what they "feel in their hearts" is right?

WHO, OR WHAT, IS THE AUTHORITY IN RELIGION?

Who has the right to offer commands, and to make laws, regarding how we should live our lives, or how we should worship? Who has moral and legal supremacy in regard to these things?

God is the primary source of religious and moral authority. When Jesus was on trial before Pilate and He refused to answer a question, Pilate said, "I have the right to put you to death." Jesus said, "You could have no power at all, except it had been given to you from above," which simply means that God is the source of all authority and power.

James Meadows
Bible Instructor and Minister

In Acts 17:24, the Bible says that God is the ultimate Authority. He is the Lord of this Earth. He created this Earth. Mankind and all the animals are subject to Him, to His decrees, and to His issuances. Psalm 95:5-6 indicates that the Earth belongs to Him. It is His house, and He is its Creator. Therefore, all who live in this house are subject to His commands and His decrees.

Ben Moseley
University Professor and Minister

Take, for example, a house that you built with your own hands—a house that you created and furnished with your own money, and where you and your family live. Would you not have the right to establish the rules about what could, and could not, be done *in* the house or *to* the house? Would you not have the right to establish some rules and guidelines for those living within your house? Certainly you would! And those living in your house would not have the right to change or alter the rules without your permission.

In a similar way, God sets the rules and guidelines for each of us. He built this world. He is the Creator of the Universe. It is *His* house, and *He* has set the rules. The house belongs to Him. It is not up to us to change the rules about living in that house. He is the Owner, Builder, and Sustainer of this great and wonderful creation. He therefore has the right to govern the affairs of men because He has *all* authority.

Now, let us go back to the Bible to see what it has to say about the authority of God. As we do, let us see who else has authority over all the creation.

   God, who at various times and in various ways spoke in time past to the fathers by the prophets, has in these last days spoken to us by His *Son, whom He has appointed heir of all things, through whom also He made the worlds (Hebrews 1:1-2).*

According to these verses, God has chosen to govern and command His creation today through His Son, Jesus Christ. According to Hebrews 1:2, God has appointed Jesus *"heir of all things."* As the only true Son of God, Christ has been given all things by God. This truth is further illustrated in John 3:35: "The Father loves the Son, and has given all things into His hand." *All* things have been given into the hands of Jesus. One of those things has to do with authority over the creation.

> *...Father, the hour has come. Glorify Your Son, that Your Son also may glorify You, as You have given Him authority over all flesh, that He should give eternal life to as many as You have given Him (John 17:1-2).*

From these verses, and others that we have examined, we can learn that God is indeed the ultimate Source of authority. We also learn, however, that He has given authority to His Son Jesus (He has "given all things into His hand," John 3:35).

> **Christ is our authority in religion. In Matthew 28:18-19, Christ said, "All authority has been given to Me in heaven and on earth. Go therefore and make disciples of all the nations."**
>
> **Curtis Cates**
> **Bible Instructor and Minister**

But what *specific* things has God given into the hands of Christ?

> *And what is the exceeding greatness of His power toward us who believe, according to the working of His mighty power which He worked in Christ when He raised Him from the dead and seated Him at His right hand in the heavenly places, far above all principality and power and might and dominion, and every name that is named, not only in this age but also in that which is to come. And He put all things under His feet, and gave Him to be head over all things to the church, which is His body, the fullness of Him who fills all in all (Ephesians 1:19-23).*

According to what we have just read, Jesus has *all* authority.

- He has authority over all principalities.
- He is above every name.
- All things are placed under His feet.
- He is the Head of the church.

Clearly, Jesus has *all* authority. This authority is something that He likewise claimed for Himself, as Matthew 28:18 makes clear: "All authority has been given to Me in heaven and on earth."

How much authority does Jesus have? He possesses *all* of it. Thus, in answering the second question about *who* is the authority in religion, we must emphatically say that *God* is the ultimate authority over the Universe, and that He has given this authority to His Son, *Jesus.*

> **Christ is our authority in religion, as Matthew 28:18 shows. Christ said, "All authority has been given to Me in heaven and on earth." God said, in speaking of Jesus, that He is His beloved Son, and that men are to hear Him (Matthew 17:5).**
>
> **Bobby Liddell**
> **Bible Instructor and Minister**

SECTION REVIEW: *WHO, OR WHAT, IS THE AUTHORITY IN RELIGION?*

Answers to the following questions can be found in the section above.

STUDY QUESTIONS

1. According to the verses below, did God build or "make" you? YES / NO

   For the LORD is the great God, And the great King above all gods. In His hand are the deep places of the earth; The heights of the hills are His also. The sea is His, for He made it; And His hands formed the dry land. Oh come, let us worship and bow down; Let us kneel before the LORD our Maker (Psalm 95:3-6).

2. According to the verse below, since God created everything, is He Lord (have all authority) over heaven and earth? YES / NO

   God, who made the world and everything in it, since He is Lord of heaven and earth, does not dwell in temples made with hands (Acts 17:24).

3. Does God have the right to establish laws regarding how we should live while dwelling upon the Earth that He created? YES / NO

4. According to Matthew 28:18, does Jesus have authority over heaven and earth? YES / NO

5. According to John 17:1-2 and the verse below, Who gave Jesus all authority? _____ _____

   The Father loves the Son, and has given all things into His hand (John 3:35).

6. According to Ephesians 1:19-23, Jesus has power (authority) over the _____, "which is His body, the fullness of Him who fills all in all."

An ANSWER KEY for the STUDY QUESTIONS is provided in the back of the book.

DECISION POINTS

A. Do you believe that God is "Lord of heaven and earth"? YES / NO

B. Are you willing to obey Jesus in whatever He tells you to do? YES / NO

TALKING POINTS

A. If you paid for, built, and owned a house, then that would give you the right to say what happened to, or in, that house. How does that principle apply to God, Who "built" the Universe?

B. According to the verse below, God commands all men everywhere to repent of their sins. Why does He have the right to issue such a command? What should the response of people on the Earth be to God's command?

   Truly, these times of ignorance God overlooked, but now commands all men everywhere to repent (Acts 17:30).

HOW IS THIS AUTHORITY MADE KNOWN?

Now let us ask: "How is this authority made known?" In other words, how does Christ govern His creation? How does He enact His laws upon that creation? Let's return for just a moment to our discussion of sports. Let's say that you or I were going to participate in an athletic event. In order to do that, would we not need to know what the rules are? Of course we would. But just knowing who the authority figure is, or who the authoritative board is, would clearly not be enough. We would need some form of communication from that authoritative figure in order to know how we are to play the game—just like the International Olympic Committee when its members communicate the rules to the players, coaches, judges, and nations.

Likewise, in dealing with religious matters, knowing that God is the Ultimate Authority is absolutely necessary. But that, in and of itself, is not sufficient. In running the race of life, we must know what the rules are. We must know what Jesus wants us to do. Remember what Jesus said in Matthew 7:21—"Not everyone who says to Me, 'Lord, Lord,' shall enter the kingdom of heaven, but he who does the will of My Father in heaven." Thus, we must know what God's rules and commandments are—the rules and commandments that have been given by God to His Son Jesus.

But how does Jesus give His commands? How does He exercise His authority? How does Jesus "move us" to do something He wants us to do? How does He communicate to us His will? Does He come to us in a dream? Does He fill our hearts with an important message?

To be certain, at one time God *did* communicate His will for human beings in some very special ways. For example, God spoke to Moses directly through a burning bush (Exodus 3:4). He also communicated through dreams, as in the case of Jacob (Genesis 31:11). Once, during a feast sponsored by a Babylonian king, God used a detached human hand to write an important message upon a wall (Daniel 5:5). On another occasion, God allowed a donkey to speak to a prophet by the name of Balaam (Numbers 22:28). But is this how God makes known His will *today*? Are these still the means by which He commands and directs us today? The Bible provides the answer.

God, who at various times and in various ways spoke in time past to the fathers by the prophets, has in these last days spoken to us by His Son, whom He has appointed heir of all things, through whom also He made the worlds (Hebrews 1:1-2).

About Authority in Religion

Yes, at one time God spoke in various ways and in different manners. But according to Hebrews 1:1-2, *today* He speaks to us through His Son. It is through Jesus Christ that we come to know the rules and commandments of God.

While Jesus was upon the Earth, He gave those rules and commandments by word of mouth—that is, according to the spoken word. According to Mark 1:38, a primary part the Lord's public ministry was given over to preaching and teaching. Jesus was very compassionate. He was very concerned about people, and wanted them to know how to be happy. Thus, He taught them the words and commandments of God. Christ's preaching was at times both compassionate and provocative, but it also was *authoritative.*

The sermons He preached spoke directly to the people as He called upon people to turn from their ungodly behavior and to abandon unauthorized religious traditions. He gave specific commandments about how to live and how to avoid sin. He variously taught such things as:

- "Do not swear" (Matthew 5:34).
- "Love your enemies" (Matthew 5:44).
- "Beware of the leaven of the Pharisees" (Matthew 16:6).
- "Love the Lord your God" (Matthew 22:37).
- "Seek first the kingdom of God" (Matthew 6:33).
- "Seek and you will find" (Matthew 7:7).
- "Enter by the narrow gate" (Matthew 7:13).
- "Beware of false prophets" (Matthew 7:15).
- "Give, and it will be given to you" (Luke 6:38).

His powerful words were received with awe and amazement, as was revealed by Matthew in regard to Christ's Sermon on the Mount.

And so it was, when Jesus had ended these sayings, that the people were astonished at His teaching, for He taught them as one having authority, and not as the scribes (Matthew 7:28-29).

Truly, the spoken words of Christ were *authoritative.* With His words, Jesus could calm a raging storm (Mark 4:39), cleanse a leper (Matthew 8:3), or raise the dead (John 11:43). Yet, notice also what Jesus says about the power and the necessity of His words for transforming the lives of sinners.

It is the Spirit who gives life; the flesh profits nothing. The words that I speak to you are spirit, and they are life (John 6:63).

The *words* of Jesus are powerful. While He was here on Earth, He called upon sinners to conform to His will. He did that by means of the spoken word. Through His preaching and teaching, He commanded people to conform to the ultimate authority of Heaven itself. He commanded the people of *that* day by His *spoken* words.

But, what about *today?* If, while upon the Earth, Jesus exercised His authority by means of the *spoken* word, how does He exercise His authority today? Since He no longer is with us in a bodily form, who or what is our authority?

In answering this question, let's read what the New Testament writers taught about the origin and authorship of their own writings:

But I make known to you, brethren, that the gospel which was preached by me is not according to man. For I neither received it from man, nor was I taught it, but it came through the revelation of Jesus Christ (Galatians 1:11-12).

Note that the apostle John was instructed by Jesus to write to the seven churches of Asia:

I was in the Spirit on the Lord's Day, and I heard behind me a loud voice, as of a trumpet, saying, "I am the Alpha and the Omega, the First and the Last," and, "What you see, write in a book and send it to the seven churches which are in Asia..." (Revelation 1:10-11).

John was told by Jesus to write down what he had seen. He and other writers of the New Testament were charged with writing down the revelation of Jesus Christ. However, it is important to know that when these men wrote the Bible, they did so under the direction and guidance of the Holy Spirit.

Knowing this first, that no prophecy of Scripture is of any private interpretation, for prophecy never came by the will of man, but holy men of God spoke as they were moved by the Holy Spirit (2 Peter 1:20-21).

These verses, and others like them, are but a few of the many references which reveal that what was written in the Bible are *not the words of men,* but instead *are the words and will of Jesus Christ,* as revealed by God's Holy Spirit.

All prophets (that is, all those who wrote the Bible) were led by the Holy Spirit. They were "carried along" in their writings so that what we have in the Bible is God's breath, God's commands, and His rule for our lives.

Chuck Horner
Bible Instructor and Minister

In the Lord's absence, He has given us the *written* word to govern our actions and guide our steps. The New Testament is the Lord's authoritative document that must be obeyed and followed. Paul, in 1 Corinthians 9:21, spoke of it as "a law," and in Galatians 6:2, identified that law as "the law of Christ" that must be "fulfilled" (i.e., obeyed). It is, as Paul revealed in Galatians 6:16, God's "rule," or standard, by which men are to live if they want to obtain the peace and mercy of God.

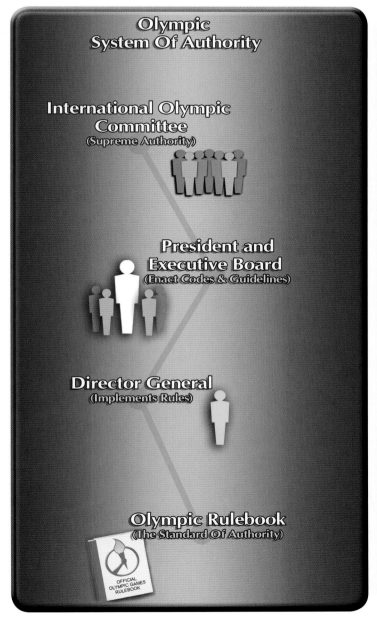

Let us return once again to the analogy of the Olympic Games. Notice again how the authority of the International Olympic Committee is exercised, and ultimately manifested, in the Olympic rulebook. If an athlete or judge wants to know what can and cannot be done, then he or she must consult the rulebook in order to be accepted and recognized by the authoritative body of the International Olympic Committee.

In the Olympic Games, the official rulebook must be consulted, studied, and obeyed in order to participate successfully in any event. Likewise, in living acceptably before God, both the individual and the church must consult, study, and obey the New Tes-

tament of Christ in order to live the Christian life successfully. According to what the apostle Paul wrote in a letter to Timothy, if we want to win the prize of heaven, we must live life according to the rules established by God.

> *You therefore must endure hardship as a good soldier of Jesus Christ. No one engaged in warfare entangles himself with the affairs of* this *life, that he may please him who enlisted him as a soldier. And also if anyone competes in athletics, he is not crowned unless he competes according to the rules (2 Timothy 2:3-5).*

In religious matters, God (i.e., the Godhead) is the Supreme Authority over all things. Jesus, as a part of the Godhead, has been given "all authority in heaven and on Earth" (Matthew 28:18). While on Earth, Jesus promised that the Holy Spirit would be sent in the name of Christ to direct the apostles in the writing of the Holy Scriptures. The Scriptures—what we know today as the Bible—are God's revelation to man. The Bible has been given to us as a rulebook or guide by which we are to live, and so we can know the rules of God, Who is our Supreme Authority.

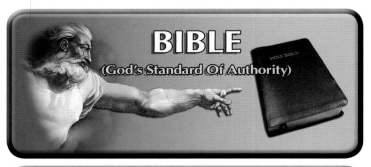

Today, *the Bible* is where we find the rules for running the *Christian* race. It is the rulebook that you and I must follow if we want to go to heaven. If we reject the rules that are found within the Bible, and if we refuse to discipline ourselves in "running the race," then we can be disqualified. This is the very point the apostle Paul was making when he said, "I discipline my body and bring it into subjection, lest, when I have preached to others, I myself should become disqualified" (1 Corinthians 9:27). The rulebook to be used to judge whether or not we will be disqualified is the New Testament of Jesus Christ. Christ Himself said:

> He who rejects Me, and does not receive My words, has that which judges him—the word that I have spoken will judge him in the last day (John 12:48).

According to Jesus, His word—as revealed in the New Testament—will be that which will judge each and every one of us at the end of the world. Today, Jesus *still* has *all authority,* and His written testament is revealed in the New Testament, which governs us even now.

Thus, in answering the third question, "How is this authority made known?," we obviously must come to the conclusion that God reveals His authority through the written word, the Bible. The Bible, therefore, should be considered the sole source for determining what is right and wrong. The Bible contains God's rules and guidelines for living the Christian life. It contains both His story of love and His commandments for life.

SECTION REVIEW: *HOW IS THIS AUTHORITY MADE KNOWN?*
Answers to the following questions can be found in the section above.

STUDY QUESTIONS

1. In the past, God communicated with His people through various means (dreams, burning bushes, talking animals, etc.). According to Hebrews 1:1-2, does God still use those means to talk to His people today? YES / NO

2. According to Hebrews 1:1-2, God has spoken to people today by _____ _____.

3. According to the verses below, do we today come to know the commandments of God through Jesus Christ? YES / NO

    He who rejects Me, and does not receive My words, has that which judges him—the word that I have spoken will judge him in the last day. For I have not spoken on My own authority; but the Father who sent Me gave Me a command, what I should say and what I should speak. And I know that His command is everlasting life. Therefore, whatever I speak, just as the Father has told Me, so I speak (John 12:48-50).

4. According to Matthew 7:28-29, are Jesus' words authoritative? YES / NO

5. While on Earth, Jesus exercised His authority by means of His *spoken* word, but today He exercises His authority by means of His _____ word, the Bible.

6. According to 2 Peter 1:20-21, the men who wrote the Bible did so under the direction and guidance of the _____ _____.

7. According to the verse below, the written revelation of Christ is also referred to as the _____ of _____.

   Bear one another's burdens, and so fulfill the law of Christ (Galatians 6:2).

8. In running the Christian race, the Bible is the _____ you and I must follow if we want to go to heaven.

9. According to 1 Corinthians 9:27, can a Christian become disqualified from reaching heaven? YES / NO

10. According to John 12:48, on the day of judgment we will be judged by the words of _____.

11. According to the verse below, do Jesus' words have the power to cleanse us from sin? YES / NO

    You are already clean because of the word which I have spoken to you (John 15:3).

12. According to John 6:63, Jesus' words are _____ and _____.

An ANSWER KEY for the STUDY QUESTIONS is provided in the back of the book.

DECISION POINTS

A. Do you believe that Jesus Christ has authority over *your* life? YES / NO

B. Are you willing to obey God's rules and commandments? YES / NO

C. Do you accept Jesus as the Head of the church? YES / NO

TALKING POINTS

A. If Jesus is the Head of the church, what does that say about churches that have men, women, or groups of people as their heads?

B. According to the verses below, name four specific things over which God gave Christ authority.

   And what is the exceeding greatness of His power toward us who believe, according to the working of His mighty power which He worked in Christ when He raised Him from the dead and seated Him at His right hand in the heavenly places, far above all principality and power and might and dominion, and every name that is named, not only in this age but also in that which is to come. And He put all things under His feet, and gave Him to be head over all things to the church, which is His body, the fullness of Him who fills all in all (Ephesians 1:19-23).

About Authority in Religion

IS THERE MORE THAN ONE STANDARD OF AUTHORITY TODAY?

Now, however, let us ask the question: "Is the Bible the only rule-book we need?" Is there more than one standard of authority today? Are there other religious groups that use something in addition to, or in place of, the New Testament? Let a theologian answer that question:

> Some put more emphasis on the Bible than others do. Some put more emphasis on something in the past, something written by men, something said by men, or something agreed upon by men. I have in my possession two books that would say much the same that we are talking about here. One book, *The Book of Discipline,* comes from a particular religious body, and says, "This *Discipline* is the book of Law of The [Church]. It is the product of many General Conferences of historical religious bodies, which now form the Church. The *Discipline* is the instrument for setting forth the laws, plan, polity, and process by which the [Churches] govern themselves." This is a book that is in addition to the Bible. It is a more common practice for some in religion to acknowledge a source of authority other than the Bible, than it is for them to acknowledge the Bible alone as the source of authority. In a book titled *Articles of Faith,* we read the following: "The Standard Works of the Church constitute the written authority of the Church in Doctrine. The works adopted by the vote of the church as authoritative in faith and doctrine are four...." The *Articles of Faith* goes on to mention four different books. The Bible is only *one* of those books. So, yes, a lot of religious groups have their own books, their own rules, and their own laws. The question we need to be asking is: "Do we really *need* those other books?" No, we do not. We have exactly what we need in the Bible.
>
> Carl Garner
> Bible Instructor and Minister

Yes, there are religious groups that use something other than the New Testament as a standard of authority in religious matters. They offer:

- Creed books
- Disciplines
- Articles of Faith
- "Other" testaments
- Conventions
- Confessions of Faith

Do we really need these other standards of authority? Can we go to the Bible alone to know what we need to do to be complete before God? Can we, by reading *just* the Bible, know such things as how to organize the church, what we should teach, and how we should worship? Can we, by a careful study of the word of God, learn what it means to be a good husband, wife, or parent? Can we, through the word of God, learn how to cope with our problems and overcome our difficulties? The apostle Paul answered such questions when he wrote:

> *All Scripture* is *given by inspiration of God, and* is *profitable for doctrine, for reproof, for correction, for instruction in righteousness, that the man of God may be complete, thoroughly equipped for every good work (2 Timothy 3:16-17).*

Yes, the Scriptures *can* make us complete before God. Indeed, they *must* be used for:

- Doctrine (teaching)
- Reproof (exposing error)
- Correction
- Instruction in righteousness (instruction in what is right or wrong)
- Instruction for every good work

Is it any wonder, then, that Peter would say about God that "His divine power has given to us *all things that pertain to life and godliness,* through the knowledge of Him who called us by glory and virtue" (2 Peter 1:3)? No, we should not be at all surprised to know that the Bible is sufficient for guiding our steps. After all, the Bible is the product of an all-knowing, all-loving God Who wants to save us and Who *wants* us to be happy!

But you might ask, "Hasn't the Spirit given 'additional revelations' since the time of the apostles? Isn't the Spirit revealing messages to us today, separate and apart from the word?"

Notice what Jesus said about the Spirit (Whom He called "the Spirit of truth"):

> *But the Helper, the Holy Spirit, whom the Father will send in My name, He will teach you all things, and bring to your remembrance all things that I said to you (John 14:26).*
>
> *...When He, the Spirit of truth, has come, He will guide you*

into all truth; for He will not speak on His own authority, but whatever He hears He will speak; and He will tell you things to come (John 16:13).

In considering these passages, there are two important truths to keep in mind:

- The apostles would be guided by the Holy Spirit in remembering the words of Christ.
- The apostles would be taught "all things," remember "all things," and be guided into "all truth."

If the apostles were guided into all truth, then should we *expect* to receive any additional revelations today? No, because *all* means *all—everything. All* the truth was delivered. According to the Bible, *all* religious truth was revealed within the lifetimes of the apostles. "The faith," as Jude revealed, "was *once for all* delivered to the saints" (Jude 3). The faith was not *partially* delivered in the first century, and then finalized several centuries later. Rather, Jude says it was *once for all* delivered. All religious truth was revealed in the first century, and no other Gospel is to be preached, as Paul made clear when he wrote:

But even if we, or an angel from heaven, preach any other gospel to you than what we have preached to you, let him be accursed (Galatians 1:8).

Paul says that *even if an angel from heaven* preaches something other than what those first-century Christians had received, it is to be rejected. Therefore, we must conclude that the Gospel—the revelation of Jesus Christ as it was given during the lifetimes of the apostles—is the *only* standard of religious authority for us today.

SECTION REVIEW: *IS THERE MORE THAN ONE STANDARD OF AUTHORITY TODAY?*

Answers to the following questions can be found in the section above.

STUDY QUESTIONS

1. Do some religious and Christian based groups use something other than the Bible and/or something in addition to the Bible as their standard for religious authority? YES / NO

2. According to the verse below, does the Bible thoroughly furnish us unto every good work? YES / NO

   All Scripture is given by inspiration of God, and is profitable for doctrine, for reproof, for correction, for instruction in righteousness, that the man of God may be complete, thoroughly equipped for every good work (2 Timothy 3:16-17).

3. According to 2 Timothy 3:16-17, do we need church traditions, manuals, creed books, confessions of faith, or a latter day revelation to make us complete before God? YES / NO

4. According to 2 Peter 1:3, "His divine power has given to us all things that pertain to _____ and _____."

5. In light of your answers to questions 3 and 4 above, do we need "other books" or any source, other than the Bible, as a standard for religious authority? YES / NO

6. According to John 16:13, in the first century Jesus told the apostles that they would be guided into _____ truth.

7. If the apostles were guided into all the truth, should we expect to receive any new revelations today? YES / NO

8. According to Galatians 1:8, Paul said "but even if we, or an angel from heaven, preach any other gospel to you than what we have preached to you, let him be _____."

9. According to Jude 3, we should "contend earnestly for the faith which was _____ _____ _____ delivered to the saints."

An ANSWER KEY for the STUDY QUESTIONS is provided in the back of the book.

DECISION POINTS

A. Do you believe that the Bible is the inspired word of God? YES / NO

B. Do you think that people today need something "in addition to" the Bible in order to go to heaven? YES / NO

C. Are you willing to do what the Bible says you need to do to be saved from your sins? YES / NO

TALKING POINTS

A. According to 2 Timothy 3:16-17, there are five things for which the Scriptures are valuable. What are those five things?

B. Why have men, or groups of men, produced other "authoritative" religious books?

WHAT IS THE DIFFERENCE BETWEEN THE OLD TESTAMENT AND THE NEW TESTAMENT?

Now that we have learned that God, through His Son Jesus, is the ultimate source of authority, and His Holy word, the Bible, is the standard for religious authority today, let's spend just a few moments talking about the Bible and its two testaments. In our search for truth about authority in religion, you may have noticed that we have, in relationship to the Bible as a whole, pointed only to the New Testament as our authority. Consequently, you might be wondering whether or not the Old Testament is important. After all, the Old Testament is the word of God, too, is it not? It certainly is. The Old Testament is just as much a part of the Bible as the New Testament, and it must be studied carefully along with the New Testament. The apostle Paul said that the Old Testament was "written for our learning, that we through the patience and comfort of the Scriptures might have hope" (Romans 15:4).

But did you ever wonder why is it called the *Old* Testament? And, is the Old Testament the religious law that we must follow today? Let a Bible instructor and specialist in Old Testament studies respond to that question.

When we speak of the Old Testament as "old," we don't mean that it is no longer useful or that it doesn't have any value. Rather, it's like when you re-write a contract. You say that you have an "old contract" and that you have a "new contract." God has made a new covenant—or new contract, if you will—with His people. And that is what the writer of the book of Hebrews discusses—that we have transitioned from a law that was specifically for the Jews (as explained in Deuteronomy 5, when God explained that the law was for the people who were present at the giving of the law on Mt. Sinai). In Jeremiah 31:31-34, God said through His prophet Jeremiah that He was going to bring about a new covenant (or new testament or new will). In Hebrews 8:13, the writer of the book of Hebrews actually quotes that passage from Jeremiah 31 in order to talk about how we are now under a new covenant. Thus, all people today are accountable to the law of Christ.

Denny Petrillo, Ph.D.
Professor of Old Testament and Judaic Studies

In summary, we can see that the Old Testament is called "old" because it is the law that no longer is in force. According to the Bible, that law was given to Israel. It was a temporary law that prepared the way, and laid the foundation, for the New Covenant given by Christ. The apostle Paul put it like this:

Therefore the law was our tutor to bring us to Christ, that we might be justified by faith. But after faith has come, we are no longer under a tutor (Galatians 3:24-25).

We no longer are under a tutor or schoolmaster. In the first century, a tutor was often a trusted slave who was responsible for caring for a child's moral and educational welfare. As part of his duty, he had the job of leading the child to and from school, and helping him grow into adulthood. Once the child became an adult, he no longer needed (or was under the authority of) the tutor. In the context of the epistle to the Galatians, the Old Testament was the tutor or schoolmaster. That law was responsible for preparing mankind for adulthood. Its purpose was to point us to Christ, and to the system of faith established by Christ. In Galatians 6:2 and 1 Corinthians 9:21, that system is referred to as "the law of Christ." That law—the law of Christ—is the law that is spiritually binding upon us today. Thus, we no longer are under the authority of the Old Testament. The Old Testament was a tutor that pointed to Jesus.

But does this mean that we are not under the Ten Commandments as contained in the book of Exodus? Strictly speaking, no, we are not. The Ten Commandments were a part of the Old Law, and that Law was abolished by Jesus. Read Ephesians 2:15—"Having abolished in His flesh the enmity, that is, the law of commandments con-

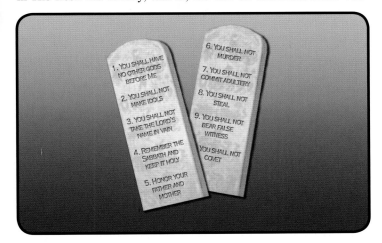

tained in ordinances, so as to create in Himself one new man from the two, thus making peace." The Ten Commandments—along with the Levitical system of blood sacrifices, tabernacle worship, the burning of incense, and special feast days—were temporary in nature. According to Hebrews 10:1, those things were a shadow of good things to come. The Old Law prepared the Israelites, and all humanity, for the coming of the Messiah and His New Covenant.

When Jesus came and brought the New Covenant, the Old Law was taken away. According to the book of Hebrews, that Law was vanishing away because it had been made "old" by the New Testament of Christ:

> *In that He says, "A new covenant," He has made the first obsolete. Now what is becoming obsolete and growing old is ready to vanish away (Hebrews 8:13).*

Today, since the Old Testament is obsolete, is it acceptable to commit adultery, to lie, or to steal? Certainly not! Nine of the Ten Commandments can be found in the New Testament. The one exception is the commandment for the Israelites to keep the Sabbath. In contrast to the Sabbath, Christians keep the Supper of the Lord. This Supper was instituted by Jesus in Matthew 26:26-28, and was observed by first-century disciples each first day of the week, according to Acts 20:7. Nine of the Ten Commandments can be found within the New Testament, and are an integral part of the New Covenant of Christ.

This New Testament, or "New Covenant of Christ," was made known by the Holy Spirit to the Lord's apostles and/or disciples. The Old Testament (in passages such as Jeremiah 31, and elsewhere) foretold of the days in which a *New* Covenant would be established. Today, that Covenant has been established. The Old Covenant has been abolished. Today, we live under the authority of Christ and His written word.

SECTION REVIEW: *WHAT IS THE DIFFERENCE BETWEEN THE OLD TESTAMENT AND THE NEW TESTAMENT?*

Answers to the following questions can be found in the section above.

STUDY QUESTIONS

1. Is the Old Testament the word of God? YES / NO

2. According to Romans 15:4, the things written in the Old Testament were written for _____ _____.

3. According to the verse below, Jesus said he did not come to destroy the Law or the Prophets, but to _____ them.

   Do not think that I came to destroy the Law or the Prophets. I did not come to destroy but to fulfill (Matthew 5:17).

4. According to the verse below, God prophesied that the days were coming when he would make a _____ _____ with the house of Israel and with the house of Judah.

   Behold, the days are coming, says the LORD, when I will make a new covenant with the house of Israel and with the house of Judah (Jeremiah 31:31).

5. According to Hebrews 8:13, "in that He says, 'a new covenant,' He has made the first obsolete. Now what is becoming obsolete and growing old is ready to _____ _____."

6. The Old Testament is called "old" because it is the _____ no longer in _____.

7. According to Galatians 3:24-25, the Old Testament law served as a _____ in preparing the world for Christ.

8. According to the verse below, do we today live under a "New Law"—the "law of Christ?" YES / NO

   And to the Jews I became as a Jew, that I might win Jews; to those who are under the law, as under the law, that I might win those who are under the law; to those who are without law, as without law (not being without law toward God, but under law toward Christ), that I might win those who are without law (1 Corinthians 9:20-21).

9. According to Ephesians 2:15, did Jesus abolish the Old Testament law of commandments? YES / NO

10. Are some of the original Ten Commandments from the Old Testament also found in the New Testament? YES / NO

11. Are there any of the original Ten Commandments that are *not* found in the New Testament? YES / NO

12. If so, which one(s)? _____ _____ _____

13. The Old Testament foretold of the days a New Covenant would be established. Today, we live under the _____ of Christ and His _____ word.

An ANSWER KEY for the STUDY QUESTIONS is provided in the back of the book.

DECISION POINTS

A. Do you believe that people today are to live *only* under the New Testament? YES / NO

B. Are you willing to do what God has told you to do in the New Testament to be saved? YES / NO

TALKING POINTS

A. Hebrews 10:1 states, "For the law, having a shadow of the good things to come, and not the very image of the things, can never with these same sacrifices, which they offer continually year by year, make those who approach perfect." In what ways was the Law "a shadow of good things to come?" What does the phrase mean?

B. While Jesus did not come to destroy the Old Testament Law, He nevertheless abolished the law (Ephesians 2:15) when he fulfilled it. How is this possible? Was the Old Testament Law temporary?

CONCLUSION

Our search for truth has led us to conclude:

1. The word "authority" means the right to rule or govern.
2. God is the ultimate Source of authority.
3. God has given Christ Jesus all authority in heaven and on Earth.
4. The New Testament of Christ is the law by which all men should live today.
5. Christ makes known His authority, and reveals His will for us, by means of the written word, the Bible.

That written word is all-sufficient for guiding us to heaven. It explains the rules for living here on this Earth. It also, according to the apostle Peter and the apostle Paul, is what we need to sustain us in our spiritual growth.

As newborn babes, desire the pure milk of the word, that you may grow thereby (1 Peter 2:2).

So then faith comes by hearing, and hearing by the word of God (Romans 10:17).

If you want to grow spiritually, you *must* study the word of God. If you want to know the rules for running the Christian race, then you *must* study the Bible. In this section, we have learned the truth about who or what our authority in religion must be. That authority is God. He has revealed His message and His guidelines in the New Testament (the New Covenant) for determining the boundaries of living the Christian life. The words of Christ will be the sole standard for judgment on the day that Christ returns, according to John 12:48.

I hope you will continue with me as we walk on this journey, searching for truth. It is the most important journey of your life. Join me as we search for truth.

exercises His authority through His _____ word, the Bible.

3. According to 2 Peter 1:3, God's word gives us all things that pertain to _____ and _____.

FOCUS QUESTIONS

1. Do we live under the Old Testament today? YES / NO

2. According to Galatians 1:8, should we be willing to accept any Gospel other than that which is presented in the New Testament? YES / NO

3. According to the verses below, the truth can be found in Jesus' _____.

…If you abide in My word, you are My disciples indeed. And you shall know the truth, and the truth shall make you free (John 8:31-32).

An ANSWER KEY for the STUDY QUESTIONS and FOCUS QUESTIONS is provided in the back of the book.

THINGS YOU SHOULD KNOW

- The word "authority" means the right to rule or govern.
- God is the ultimate Source of authority.
- Jesus received all authority from God.
- Jesus is the Head of the church.
- We will be judged by the teachings of Jesus.
- The Apostles were inspired by the Holy Spirit in their writing of the Bible.
- The inspired word is our only guide in religion.
- The New Testament is the law which we are under and by which we will be judged.

CHAPTER REVIEW

Answers to the following questions can be found within this chapter.

STUDY QUESTIONS

1. According to Matthew 28:18, Jesus said "_____ authority has been given to Me in heaven and on earth."

2. While Jesus was upon the Earth, He exercised His authority and gave His commandments through His *spoken* words. Today, Jesus

DIGGING DEEPER…

The material below is intended for those people who would like to study this subject further. It contains information that was not necessarily discussed in the lesson.

 GOD AS THE SOURCE OF TRUTH

He is *the Rock, His work* is *perfect; For all His ways* are *justice, A God of truth and without injustice; Righteous and upright* is *He (Deuteronomy 32:4).*

The Spirit of the LORD spoke by me, And His word was *on my tongue (2 Samuel 23:2).*

The entrance of Your words gives light; It gives understanding to the simple (Psalm 119:130).

The entirety of Your word is *truth, And every one of Your righteous judgments* endures *forever (Psalm 119:160).*

Your words were found, and I ate them, And Your word was to me the joy and rejoicing of my heart; For I am called by Your name, O LORD God of hosts (Jeremiah 15:16).

Sanctify them by Your truth. Your word is truth (John 17:17).

Now we have received, not the spirit of the world, but the Spirit who is from God, that we might know the things that have been freely given to us by God. These things we also speak, not in words which man's wisdom teaches but which the Holy Spirit teaches, comparing spiritual things with spiritual (1 Corinthians 2:12-13).

Paul, a bondservant of God and an apostle of Jesus Christ, according to the faith of God's elect and the acknowledgment of the truth which accords with godliness, in hope of eternal life which God, who cannot lie, promised before time began (Titus 1:1-2).

Knowing this first, that no prophecy of Scripture is of any private interpretation, for prophecy never came by the will of man, but holy men of God spoke as they were *moved by the Holy Spirit (2 Peter 1:20-21).*

THINGS TO THINK ABOUT…WHEN DIGGING DEEPER

1. According to Deuteronomy 32:4, God is a God of _____.

2. In 2 Samuel 23:2, David says that God put His word on David's _____.

3. According to Psalm 119:130, God's words give _____ and _____.

4. According to Psalm 119:160, is all of God's word truth? YES / NO

5. In Jeremiah 15:16, did Jeremiah find joy in feasting on his own words? YES / NO

6. According to John 17:17, Jesus says God's word is _____.

7. Does 1 Corinthians 2:12-13 teach that the things the Bible writers wrote came from God? YES / NO

8. Titus 1:1-2 teaches that God cannot _____.

9. "Holy men of God _____ as they were _____ by the Holy Spirit" (2 Peter 1:20-21).

MAN'S DEPENDENCE ON GOD AND HIS WORD

How can a young man cleanse his way? By taking heed according to Your word. With my whole heart I have sought You; Oh, let me not wander from Your commandments! Your word I have hidden in my heart, That I might not sin against You (Psalm 119:9-11).

Trust in the LORD with all your heart, And lean not on your own understanding (Proverbs 3:5).

There is a way that seems right to a man, *But its end* is *the way of death (Proverbs 14:12).*

Let us hear the conclusion of the whole matter: Fear God and keep His commandments, For this is man's all (Ecclesiastes 12:13).

O LORD, I know the way of man is *not in himself; It is* not in man who *walks to direct his own steps (Jeremiah 10:23).*

Enter by the narrow gate; for wide is *the gate and broad* is *the way that leads to destruction, and there are many who go in by it. Because narrow* is *the gate and difficult* is *the way which leads to life, and there are few who find it (Matthew 7:13-14).*

Not everyone who says to Me, 'Lord, Lord,' shall enter the kingdom of heaven, but he who does the will of My Father in heaven (Matthew 7:21).

These [Christians in Berea] *were more fair-minded than those in Thessalonica, in that they received the word with all readiness, and searched the Scriptures daily* to find out *whether these things were so (Acts 17:11).*

And do not be conformed to this world, but be transformed by the renewing of your mind, that you may prove what is *that good and acceptable and perfect will of God (Romans 12:2).*

Test all things; hold fast what is good (1 Thessalonians 5:21).

Be diligent to present yourself approved to God, a worker who does not need to be ashamed, rightly dividing the word of truth (2 Timothy 2:15).

Beloved, do not believe every spirit, but test the spirits, whether they are of God; because many false prophets have gone out into the world (1 John 4:1).

…Great and marvelous are *Your works, Lord God Almighty! Just and true* are *Your ways, O King of the saints! (Revelation 15:3).*

THINGS TO THINK ABOUT...WHEN DIGGING DEEPER

10. Does Psalm 119:9-11 teach that we are dependent on God and His word to cleanse our ways and prevent sin? YES / NO

11. According to Proverbs 3:5, are we to use our own understanding to determine what is right or wrong? YES / NO

12. "There is a way that seems right to a man, But its end is the way of _____" (Proverbs 14:12).

13. According to Jeremiah 10:23, is man's way the right way? YES / NO

14. According to Matthew 7:21, can we get to heaven by doing whatever we want to do? YES / NO

15. Do 1 Thessalonians 5:21 and 1 John 4:1 teach that we are to "test" everything that we are taught in order to see if it is from God? YES / NO

16. In Acts 17:11, the Christians at Berea "tested" to see if Paul was teaching things from God by _____ _____ _____ _____.

17. Romans 12:2 teaches that we should not be conformed to the _____ but to the will of _____.

MAN'S DEPENDENCE ON JESUS

Therefore whoever hears these sayings of Mine, and does them, I will liken him to a wise man who built his house on the rock: and the rain descended, the floods came, and the winds blew and beat on that house; and it did not fall, for it was founded on the rock. But everyone who hears these sayings of Mine, and does not do them, will be like a foolish man who built his house on the sand: and the rain descended, the floods came, and the winds blew and beat on that house; and it fell. And great was its fall (Matthew 7:24-27).

...This is My beloved Son, in whom I am well pleased. Hear Him! (Matthew 17:5).

Then Jesus said to those Jews who believed Him, "If you abide in My word, you are My disciples indeed. And you shall know the truth, and the truth shall make you free." They answered Him, "We are Abraham's descendants, and have never been in bondage to anyone. How can You say, 'You will be made free'?" Jesus answered them, "Most assuredly, I say to you, whoever commits sin is a slave of sin. And a slave does not abide in the house forever, but a son abides forever. Therefore if the Son makes you free, you shall be free indeed" (John 8:31-36).

Jesus said to him, "I am the way, the truth, and the life. No one comes to the Father except through Me" (John 14:6).

And this is eternal life, that they may know You, the only true God, and Jesus Christ whom You have sent (John 17:3).

And truly Jesus did many other signs in the presence of His disciples, which are not written in this book; but these are written that you may believe that Jesus is the Christ, the Son of God, and that believing you may have life in His name (John 20:30-31).

Men of Israel, hear these words: Jesus of Nazareth, a Man attested by God to you by miracles, wonders, and signs which God did through Him in your midst, as you yourselves also know—Him, being delivered by the determined purpose and foreknowledge of God, you have taken by lawless hands, have crucified, and put to death (Acts 2:22-23).

For in Him [Christ] dwells all the fullness of the Godhead bodily (Colossians 2:9).

THINGS TO THINK ABOUT...WHEN DIGGING DEEPER

18. Does Acts 2:22-23 teach that God attested Jesus (affirmed Him to be true or genuine) through miracles, wonders, and signs that the people around him saw? YES / NO

19. According to John 17:3, eternal life comes through knowing _____ and _____ _____.

20. In Matthew 7:24-27, Jesus teaches that if we listen and obey we are _____, but if not, we are _____.

21. In Matthew 17:5, God said we must listen to Jesus. YES / NO

22. John 8:31-32 teaches that if we remain in Jesus' word, we will know the _____.

23. John 8:33-36 teaches that Jesus is able to make us _____.

24. Does John 14:6 teach that the only way to go to God the Father is through Jesus? YES / NO

An ANSWER KEY for the DIGGING DEEPER QUESTIONS is provided in the back of the book.

Searching for Truth

ABOUT THE CHURCH

The word church is used well over one hundred times in the New Testament. It is obviously a very important word but what, exactly, does it mean? Is the church merely a place for worship? Is it the sum of all the religious denominations? Or, is it something more personal and spiritual? And furthermore, how important is the church? And, does Jesus have a church to which we must belong in order to be saved?

INTRODUCTION

When you think of a church, do you think of a building? Most people do. Even the dictionary defines the word "church" as: "a building set apart or consecrated for public worship" (*Webster's New World Dictionary*).

But is the church simply a building made of wood or stone? Or is there something more? Indeed there is, for the church—as established by Jesus Christ—existed long before any building, denomination, or Christian organization came into existence. What, then, is the church and what should our attitude be toward that church? As we search through the Scriptures (the Bible—God's word, and our authoritative source for truth), let us see what we can discover about "the church."

In searching for truth about the church, we need to answer three important questions:

1. **What is the church?**
2. **Is the church essential?**
3. **Must the church be unified?**

WHAT IS THE CHURCH?

First, we need to ask, "What is the church?" The word "church" brings to mind different things for different people. The Greek word *ekklesia* is usually translated as "church," and has an important application in the realm of the New Testament.

> In most people's minds, the church is the building. The Greek word translated "church" in our English New Testament comes from a word meaning "the called out," speaking of the people. One of the best definitions I know of "the church" is found in Acts 8:1 and Acts 9:1. In Acts 8:1, it says that Paul was persecuting "the church." In Acts 9:1, we read where Paul was persecuting "the disciples of the Lord." Therefore, "the church" and "the disciples of the Lord" are the same thing.
>
> Keith Mosher Sr.
> Bible Instructor and Minister

Within the New Testament, the word "church" has both a significant meaning and well-defined parameters. It is mentioned first in Matthew's Gospel, where in chapter 16 we find Peter proclaiming Jesus as the Christ and the Son of God. In response to Peter's affirmation, let us observe what Jesus had to say:

> *And I also say to you that you are Peter, and on this rock I will build My church, and the gates of Hades shall not prevail against it. And I will give you the keys of the kingdom of heaven, and whatever you bind on earth will be bound in heaven, and whatever you loose on earth will be loosed in heaven (Matthew 16:18-19).*

As we strive to understand the meaning of the word "church," we need to notice three things concerning what Jesus said:

1. **Christ would have a church.**
2. **Jesus would be the builder of His church.**
3. **Peter (and the rest of the apostles—cf. Matthew 18:18) would be given the keys to the kingdom.**

In regard to this third point, it is important to note that *keys* are symbolic of *authority*. Approximately one year after the Lord made the promise to build His church, we find Peter and the other apostles using these keys of authority to open the doors of the kingdom at the establishment of the church.

About the Church

This event took place on the same day as the Jewish celebration of Pentecost, and is recorded by the inspired writer Luke in Acts 2. As we read through this chapter, we see that the twelve apostles were given power from on high when the Holy Spirit was poured out on them while they were waiting in a house in Jerusalem. This outpouring of the Spirit upon the apostles that had been prophesied by the prophet Joel was, among several other things, a sign that God was about to establish His kingdom (Joel 2). Having no prior learning in some of the dialects and languages mentioned in Acts 2:9-11, the apostles were nevertheless able to preach the Gospel of Christ in various human languages to the individuals represented by these various ethnic and national groups. This Gospel message consisted of: (a) a reference to Old Testament prophecies about the Holy Spirit (which were being fulfilled that very day); (b) a summary of the Lord's credentials; (c) a message about the meaning and significance of Christ's death, burial, and resurrection; and (d) the revelation about the exaltation of Jesus to David's throne. Upon hearing this sermon, sincere and conscience-pricked souls who were in need of salvation cried out in belief, asking: "Men and brethren, what shall we do?" (Acts 2:37). Here is what Peter told them to do to obtain the remission (forgiveness) of their sins:

> ...Repent, and let every one of you be baptized in the name of Jesus Christ for the remission of sins; and you shall receive the gift of the Holy Spirit. For the promise is to you and to your children, and to all who are afar off, as many as the Lord our God will call (Acts 2:38-39).

God was then, and still is today, calling all sinners to repent and be baptized. But read what Luke, the writer of the book of Acts, has to say about what happened as Peter continued his sermon.

> And with many other words he testified and exhorted them, saying, "Be saved from this perverse generation." Then those who gladly received his word were baptized; and that day about three thousand souls were added to them (Acts 2:40-41).

Notice again that sinners were told to be *baptized,* and that *baptism was "for the remission of sins."* Those who gladly accepted what Peter said were baptized, and subsequently were forgiven of their sins—just as God had promised. They were *saved.* But upon being baptized, of what did they became a part? Did they join a particular denomination? Read once more what Luke has to say as he, by the Holy Spirit, reveals what happened on that day almost two thousand years ago:

> Then those who gladly received his word were baptized; and that day about three thousand souls were added to them.... So continuing daily with one accord in the temple, and breaking bread from house to house, they ate their food with gladness and simplicity of heart, praising

> God and having favor with all the people. And the Lord added to the church daily those who were being saved (Acts 2:41, 46-47).

Did you notice what Luke said was happening? Those who were being *baptized* were being added to the number of those who were being *saved,* and those who were being *saved* were added to the *church.* They did not "join the church of their choice." Nor did they become part of a denomination, because, of course, no denominations existed at that time. Instead, as sinners were being baptized, they were being saved. At the same time, Christ was adding them to others whom He had saved. Collectively, all those saved individuals made up what was known as "the church" (Acts 2:47). To put it plainly, "the church" is the collection of all the saved, and "the saved" compose what is known as "the church." In short,

"the church" = "the saved"

Throughout the book of Acts (and the rest of the New Testament) you will see that these saved individuals are identified in exactly this way—that is, as "the church." The word "church" is used to refer to these saved individuals in one of three ways. First, "church" is used in a *local* sense (as in "the church at Jerusalem"). Second, it is used in a *universal* sense to refer to the saved all over the world (as in "Christ loved the church"). Third, it is used in a *specific* sense (as is the case when the Bible speaks of the saved coming together in an assembly for worship). In all three cases, the word "church" refers to those who have been saved.

- **Local ("the church in Jerusalem"—Acts 11:22)**
- **Universal ("Christ also loved the church"—Ephesians 5:25)**
- **Specific ("in the midst of the assembly [church] I will sing"—Hebrews 2:12)**

In a collective sense, those individuals who compose the group known as "the saved" are identified in Scripture by a number of

The Saved:
The Church
The Kingdom
The Temple
The Household
of God
The Body

meaningful and descriptive terms, each of which helps us to understand the nature and work of the saved. Some of the designations used to describe "the saved" are as follows:

The Church ("the called out," Matthew 16:18)

As the Greek word for church reveals, the saved are "the called out"—called *out* of the world of darkness, and *into* God's spiritual light (1 Peter 2:9; Colossians 1:13; Romans 13:12).

The Kingdom (Colossians 1:13)

When we think of a kingdom, we typically think of a king and loyal citizens who are servants within that kingdom. As saved individuals, Christians live under the kingship of Jesus. They are under the rule and domain of Christ the King (1 Timothy 6:15; Revelation 17:14).

The Temple (1 Corinthians 3:16)

In pagan cultures, temples are usually thought of as a dwelling place or house for a god. In the Bible, we learn that the one true living God dwells within the church. His Holy Spirit takes up His abode within each Christian (2 Corinthians 6:16).

The Household of God (Ephesians 2:19)

In the New Testament, the word "household" often refers to a family unit with a father, mother, sisters, and brothers. In a similar fashion, the church should be thought of as a family—with God as our heavenly Father, Christ as our elder Brother, and the saved as our spiritual brothers and sisters (Matthew 12:48-50; John 20:17; Hebrews 2:10-13).

The Body (Colossians 1:24)

Just as the human body has a single head but various parts, so those who are saved have as their Head Christ Jesus, with the various parts of the body being individual Christians. Just as a human body functions properly when all of its parts work together as a single unit, so the church is a single body that reveals unity and singularity (Ephesians 4:4; Romans 12:1-5; 1 Corinthians 12:12-26).

In fact, it is this last designation, the body, coupled with a reference from 1 Corinthians 12:27, that so clearly makes the point that *the church is the saved—a sanctified people belonging to Christ.* Listen to what Paul wrote to the saved in Colossae and Corinth:

> *Now you are the body of Christ, and members individually (1 Corinthians 12:27).*

> *...Fill up in my flesh what is lacking in the afflictions of Christ, for the sake of His body, which is the church (Colossians 1:24).*

The body and the church are one and the same. And because this is true, Paul was able to refer to Christians at Corinth as "the body of Christ." Those Christians in that city were known as "the church."

They were the church of Christ in that community. Thus, in answering the question, "What is the church?," we must conclude that the church is not a building or a place for worship. Rather, *the church is a group of saved people belonging to God.*

To further illustrate the nature and essence of the church, let us observe an additional passage within a letter written by the apostle Paul to a young evangelist by the name of Timothy.

> *These things I write to you, though I hope to come to you shortly; but if I am delayed, I write so that you may know how you ought to conduct yourself in the house of God, which is the church of the living God, the pillar and ground of the truth (1 Timothy 3:14-15).*

When Paul referred to "the house of God," was he speaking of a *literal* house? No! He was speaking of a *spiritual* house that is the church.

The church, God's house, was built upon the solid rock of the Lord's deity (Matthew 16:13-19). After Peter made his great confession about Christ's deity, Jesus said, "Upon this rock, I will build My church...." According to Ephesians 2:20, Jesus is the Cornerstone, and His holy apostles and prophets are the foundation. From 1 Peter 2:5, we learn that Christians are the *living stones* of which the spiritual house is composed. According to 1 Timothy 3:15, the church is "the pillar and ground of the truth." As such, the church bears the responsibility of going into all the world to preach the truth—the good news of Christ, Who is the Door by Whom men must enter to obtain eternal life. Leading up to that Door are the steps of salvation, which each sinner must climb in order to enter the church.

This, then, is the basic structure of the house of God—the collection of Christians built upon Jesus as the Cornerstone, and upon the foundation of the apostles and prophets. So again we ask, "What is the church?" The church is:

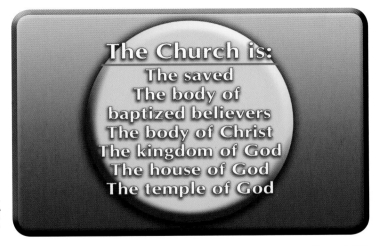

The Church is:
The saved
The body of
baptized believers
The body of Christ
The kingdom of God
The house of God
The temple of God

God's Spiritual House "THE CHURCH"

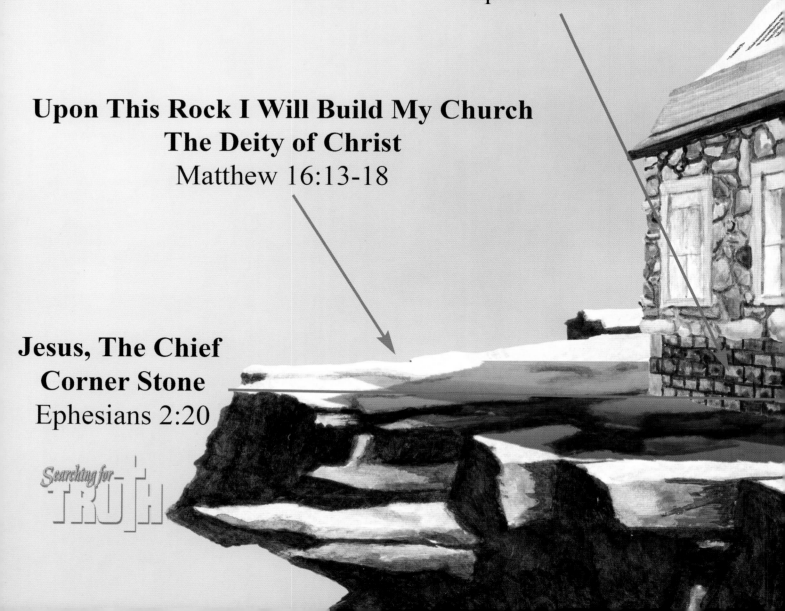

Apostles & Prophets
The Foundation
Ephesians 2:20

Upon This Rock I Will Build My Church
The Deity of Christ
Matthew 16:13-18

Jesus, The Chief
Corner Stone
Ephesians 2:20

Searching for TRUTH

The Truth
1 Timothy 3:15

**Christians
Living Stones**
1 Peter 2:5

**Jesus
The Door**
John 10:9

Baptism Mark 16:16
Confess Romans 10:9-10
Repent Luke 13:3
Believe John 8:24
Hear John 6:45

About the Church

SECTION REVIEW: *WHAT IS THE CHURCH?*

Answers to the following questions can be found in the section above.

STUDY QUESTIONS

1. The English word "church" is translated from a Greek word meaning the "_____ _____."

2. According to the verses below, are the terms "the church" and "the disciples of the Lord" one and the same? YES / NO

    Now Saul was consenting to his death. At that time a great persecution arose against the church which was at Jerusalem; and they were all scattered throughout the regions of Judea and Samaria, except the apostles (Acts 8:1).

    Then Saul, still breathing threats and murder against the disciples of the Lord, went to the high priest (Acts 9:1).

3. According to Matthew 16:18, did Jesus promise to build His church? YES / NO

4. According to Acts 2:41 and 46-47, did Christ's church begin on the Day of Pentecost following His resurrection? YES / NO

5. Did the Gospel message preached on the day of Pentecost include instruction on the meaning and significance of Christ's death, burial, and resurrection? YES / NO

6. According to Acts 2:38, on the day that Christ established His church the apostle Peter said the following, "Repent, and let every one of you be

    _____ in the name of Jesus Christ for the _____ _____ _____."

7. According to Acts 2:47, the Lord "added to the church daily those who were being _____."

8. The word "church" refers to the collection of all the _____.

9. Are phrases such as "the kingdom," "the household of God," and "the body," terms that refer to "the church"? YES / NO

10. According to 1 Timothy 3:14-15, Paul said, "I write so that you may know how you ought to conduct yourself in the _____

    _____ _____, which is the _____ of the living God, the pillar and ground of the truth."

11. According to the verses below, is the church built upon the foundation of Christ's deity (the fact that Christ is God's Son)? YES / NO

    When Jesus came into the region of Caesarea Philippi, He asked His disciples, saying, "Who do men say that I, the Son of Man, am?" So they said, "Some say John the Baptist, some Elijah, and others Jeremiah or one of the prophets." He said to them, "But who do you say that I am?" Simon Peter answered and said, "You are the Christ, the Son of the living God." Jesus answered and said to him, "Blessed are you, Simon Bar-Jonah, for flesh and blood has not revealed this to you, but My Father who is in heaven. And I also say to you that you are Peter, and on this rock I will build My church, and the gates of Hades shall not prevail against it. And I will give you the keys of the kingdom of heaven, and whatever you bind on earth will be bound in heaven, and whatever you loose on earth will be loosed in heaven" (Matthew 16:13-19).

12. According to the verse below, in referring to God's spiritual house, the church, the apostle Peter said the following, "You also, as

    _____ _____, are being built up a spiritual house, a holy priesthood."

    You also, as living stones, are being built up a spiritual house, a holy priesthood, to offer up spiritual sacrifices acceptable to God through Jesus Christ (1 Peter 2:5).

13. Examine the drawing/chart entitled *God's Spiritual House: The Church,* and answer the following questions:

    a. Who is the chief corner stone of God's house, the church? _____

b.   Who is the door through which sinners must pass in order to enter the church? _____

c.   Before entering the door, what are the steps leading to salvation/the church? _____, _____,

_____, _____, _____.

An ANSWER KEY for the STUDY QUESTIONS is provided in the back of the book.

DECISION POINTS

A.   According to Acts 2:38 and the verses below, a person must be baptized to be saved. Have you been baptized for the forgiveness of your sins? YES / NO

> *He who believes and is baptized will be saved; but he who does not believe will be condemned (Mark 16:16).*

> *There is also an antitype which now saves us—baptism (not the removal of the filth of the flesh, but the answer of a good conscience toward God), through the resurrection of Jesus Christ (1 Peter 3:21).*

B.   "The church" is composed of "the saved." Are you a member of Christ's church, and therefore saved? YES / NO

C.   Do you want to become a part of the body of Christ, the church, and thereby be saved from the consequences of sin? YES / NO

TALKING POINTS

A.   Why is it important for people who want to go to heaven to be members of Christ's church?

B.   What did Paul mean when he wrote that the church is "the pillar and ground of the truth" (1 Timothy 3:14-15)?

C.   Why do so many believe the false idea that a church is simply a building?

IS THE CHURCH ESSENTIAL AND IMPORTANT?

Now let us ask, "Is the church essential and important?" Does one *have* to be a member of the church in order to be saved? Can a person simply "have an *individual* relationship with Jesus," and not necessarily be involved in the church? Occasionally, you might hear someone say, "Give me Jesus, but not the church," or "Give me the Man, but not the plan." You also might hear someone say that it is not essential for a person to be a member of the church in order to go to heaven. But are such remarks true?

In a letter written to the church at Ephesus, the apostle Paul revealed just how essential (and valuable) the church is in regard to your relationship to God.

> *But now in Christ Jesus you who once were far off have been brought near by the blood of Christ. For He Himself is our peace, who has made both one, and has broken down the middle wall of separation, having abolished in His flesh the enmity,* that is, *the law of commandments contained in ordinances, so as to create in Himself one new man* from *the two,* thus *making peace, and that He might reconcile them both to God in one body through the cross, thereby putting to death the enmity (Ephesians 2:13-16).*

According to Paul, the division and separation that once existed between God and mankind (as well as between Jew and Gentile) have been eliminated via the church. From Isaiah 59:1-2 and Romans 6:23, we learn that sin brought about a division between God and the sinner. The Bible also teaches that because of sin, we became enemies of God. But because of the good news about Jesus and His death upon the cross, we can be both *friends of God* and *reconciled to His loving favor.*

> *For if when we were enemies we were reconciled to God through the death of His Son, much more, having been reconciled, we shall be saved by His life. And not only that,* but we also rejoice in God through our Lord Jesus

About the Church

Christ, through whom we have now received the reconciliation (Romans 5:10-11).

Webster's defines "reconcile" as: "to restore to union and friendship after estrangement." Reconciliation, therefore, is a term that refers to separate parties or factions being brought back together, and being made one. From Ephesians 2:16, we learn that reconciliation is found "in the one body" of Christ. That "body" was identified by Paul as "the church" when he said that God made Christ "the head over all things to the church, which is His body" (Ephesians 1:22-23).

"Christ's body" (of believers) and "the church" are one and the same. *Thus, if you want to be saved by being reconciled to God, you must be "in the body"—which, of course, is the same thing as saying you must be "in the church."* So, yes, if you want to be reconciled to God, you *have* to be in the Lord's body, the church. To be saved, you must be in the church.

If you continue searching through the book of Ephesians, you will discover other reasons relating to why the church is so valuable and essential. Paul wrote:

To me, who am less than the least of all the saints, this grace was given, that I should preach among the Gentiles the unsearchable riches of Christ, and to make all see what is the fellowship of the mystery, which from the beginning of the ages has been hidden in God who created all things through Jesus Christ; to the intent that now the manifold wisdom of God might be made known by the church to the principalities and powers in the heavenly places, according to the eternal purpose which He accomplished in Christ Jesus our Lord (Ephesians 3:8-11).

From this passage we can observe two important points. First, notice that *the church is an example (or reflection) of God's wisdom.* From its organization to its unique form of worship, *the church is the greatest institution ever established.* One of the things that makes it so unique is its cross-cultural and cross-national fellowship. In Ephesians, Paul revealed that a division had existed among men—a division between Jews and Gentiles. Paul referred to this division earlier in Ephesians 2:14 when he spoke of the existence of "a wall of separation."

The wall that Paul mentioned in Ephesians 2:14 was, in one sense, a literal wall. The wall had been erected within the Herodian temple complex. It was designed to prevent the Gentiles from entering into the temple sanctuary and its inner courts. What we must understand is that the Gentiles were not offered, and had not been extended, true fellowship with the Jews as a result of this barrier. Not only that, but it was symbolic of the fact that the Gentiles had not been given equal access to God and to His spiritual blessings and promises under the Old Law.

Alfred Washington
Minister

Chapter 4

The eradication of that division or "wall of separation" had been predicted by two Old Testament prophets, Isaiah and Daniel. Both had prophesied about God's plan to eradicate that wall in order to remedy the division between Jew and Gentile by means of Christ's death upon the cross, and through God's kingdom, the church.

> Paul, in Ephesians 2, conveyed the idea that through the redemptive work of Jesus Christ, this "middle wall of separation" had been removed. Now, both Jews and Gentiles have equal access to the spiritual blessings and promises of God. Regardless of nationality, social class, or political affiliation, education level, or gender, we can all have access to God through the body of Christ, which is His church.
>
> Alfred Washington
> Minister

This church, then, would be an all-inclusive body of people that would rise above both nationality and ethnicity. The church, as God's kingdom, would consist of people from all over the world. Or, as Isaiah put it, "All nations would flow into it" (Isaiah 2:2).

In the church of Christ it does not matter what color your skin is or where you were born. It does not matter whether you are male or female, rich or poor, educated or uneducated. The church is a family. The church—if it follows God's plan—is an example of how people of all nationalities and cultures can dwell together in peace and harmony.

Today, when a person (through faith in Jesus) is baptized into Christ, he or she is thereby clothed with Christ, and becomes a part of a family where divisive lines of nationality or social status are eliminated:

> For as many of you as were baptized into Christ have put on Christ. There is neither Jew nor Greek, there is neither slave nor free, there is neither male nor female; for you are all one in Christ Jesus (Galatians 3:27-28).

The church is a shining example of how God brings people together. Through baptism into Christ, people of all nations and cultures become one. They become a part of a brotherhood that is completely devoid of economic status or political standing. As a family, the church exhibits mutual care and concern for all of its members. According to the Bible, the church is a place where there exists a single heart and a generous spirit of love (Acts 2:44-46; 4:32-35). The church is a haven of happiness and good will—especially for those who have been abandoned or mistreated by their earthly families—with many brothers, sisters, fathers, and mothers to help foster and care for its spiritual children.

The church truly reflects the multifaceted wisdom of God. And we should thank God for it! But the church does not reflect merely the wisdom of God. We learn from Ephesians 3:11 that the church is essential because it has always been within the eternal purpose of God. It was in His mind long before the world was created. The church is not, as some have wrongly taught, an "afterthought" or "last-minute decision" made by the Lord when He allegedly was unable to establish an earthly kingdom.

Rather, we know from Scripture that the church was:

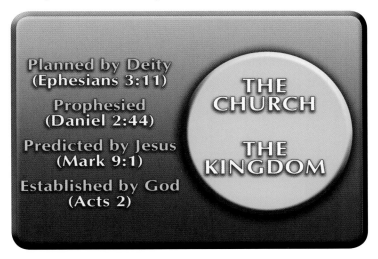

Planned by Deity (Ephesians 3:11)
Prophesied (Daniel 2:44)
Predicted by Jesus (Mark 9:1)
Established by God (Acts 2)
THE CHURCH THE KINGDOM

The church and the kingdom, as we learned earlier, are one and the same. This kingdom had been planned by Deity, prophesied by the prophets, predicted by Jesus, and established by God. This all occurred according to a master plan that saw its fulfillment in the first century, and that is still being realized today.

This kingdom, as revealed in the Bible, was in existence during the first century (Colossians 1:13; 2 Thessalonians 1:5; Revelation 1:9). According to the prophet Daniel, it was to be established during the days of the Roman Empire.

> And in the days of these kings the God of heaven will set up a kingdom which shall never be destroyed; and the kingdom shall not be left to other people; it shall break in pieces and consume all these kingdoms, and it shall stand forever (Daniel 2:44).

From the context of this passage, we learn that the phrase "in the days of these kings" clearly refers to the Roman Empire. Daniel had prophesied that four successive world empires (Babylonian, Medo-Persian, Greek, and Roman) would control the region of Palestine. It was during the fourth empire—which history records as the Roman Empire with its emperors or kings—that the church of Christ ("the kingdom of God") would be established.

The Book of Daniel & God's Kingdom
(The Church)

ANCIENT EMPIRES OF MESOPOTAMIA
AND THE MEDITERRANEAN

DANIEL'S PROPHECY
& INTERPRETATION

GOLD	**Babylonian** (625 B.C. - 539 B.C.)	"This image's head was of fine gold...The God of heaven has given you a kingdom...you [Nebuchadnezzar of Babylon] are this head of gold" (Daniel 2:32, 37, 38; cf. 1:1).
SILVER	**Medo-Persian** (539 B. C. - 331 B.C.)	"Its chest and arms of silver...after you [Nebuchadnezzar] shall arise another kingdom inferior to yours" (Daniel 2:32, 39; cf. 8:20).
BRONZE	**Greek** (331 B.C. - 63 B.C.)	"Its belly and thighs of bronze...then another, a third kingdom of bronze, which shall rule over all the earth" (Daniel 2:32, 39; cf. 8:21).
IRON & CLAY	**Roman** (146 B.C. - A.D. 476)	"Its legs of iron, its feet partly of iron and partly of clay...and the fourth kingdom shall be as strong as iron, ...that kingdom will break in pieces and crush all the others" (Daniel 2:33, 40, 42, 43).

Kingdom of God Established (approx. A.D. 33)

"And in the days of these kings the God of heaven will set up a kingdom which shall never be destroyed; and the kingdom shall not be left to other people; it shall break in pieces and consume all these kingdoms, and it shall stand forever" (Daniel 2:44).

The New Testament reveals that Jesus and John the Baptist preached the establishment of God's kingdom by saying it was "at hand" (Matthew 3:2; 4:17, 23). Since the church and the kingdom are one and the same (Matthew 16:18-19; Mark 9:1; Acts 1:3; 2:38, 47; 8:12; Colossians 1:13), and the church was established in the first century during the days of the Roman empire, it follows that the kingdom of God was established in the first century following the earthly ministry of Jesus. The church/kingdom is comprised of people from all nations (Isaiah 2:1-2) and thus consumes "all these kingdoms" (Daniel 2:44) and is spoken of in the New Testament as having been in existence during the first century A.D. (Colossians 1:13; 2 Thessalonians 1:5; Revelation 1:9). This kingdom still exists today, and all penitent sinners can choose to become a part of it by being immersed into Christ. Jesus, as the head of His church and the King of all kings (Colossians 1:18; 1 Timothy 6:15), is now reigning over His kingdom—His people (Acts 2:36; Luke 17:21).

During the first century, then, the eternal plan of God was realized. The kingdom of Christ was established. And by reading the New Testament, we can see that men and women of all nationalities were welcome into it, and became a part of it. So, truly, the church *is* important. It is an essential part of God's plan to redeem humankind.

But let us look further into the book of Ephesians in order to learn even more about the necessity and importance of the church:

> *For the husband is head of the wife, as also Christ is head of the church; and He is the Savior of the body.... Husbands, love your wives, just as Christ also loved the church and gave Himself for her (Ephesians 5:23,25).*

There are several significant truths revealed in this passage. But in light of our question about the importance of the church, let us concentrate on two important truths: Christ loves the church, and He is the Savior of the body. If Christ (our great Example) loved the church, shouldn't we love the church, too? Absolutely! The church of Jesus Christ ought to be the most important thing in our lives!

Because Christ loved the church enough to shed His blood and die on its behalf, shouldn't we want to be a part of it? Indeed we should, because as Paul wrote in 2 Timothy 2:10, "salvation...is in Christ."

Since "the body of Christ" is the same thing as "the church of Christ," would we not therefore need to be "in the church" (Christ's body) to be saved? Certainly we would! *We must be in the body of Christ to be saved.*

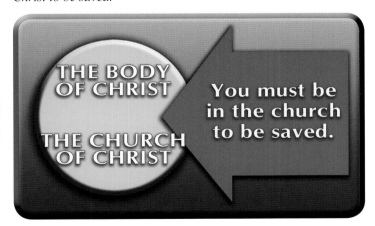

It is clear, then, that not only is the church *important* and *valuable,* but it also is *necessary* and *essential.*

Now, however, let us notice a final point from the Ephesian letter, which will bring us to our last major question.

There is *one body and one Spirit, just as you were called in one hope of your calling; one Lord, one faith, one baptism (Ephesians 4:4-5).*

After hearing Paul, we must conclude that, just as there is *only one God, one Spirit, and one faith,* there is also *only one body.* Since the body and the church are the same (as revealed in Ephesians 1:22-23), it is clear that *there is only one church.* Jesus spoke to this very fact when He said, "On this rock I will build My church, and the gates of Hades shall not prevail against it" (Matthew 16:18).

Did Jesus say that He would build *churches* (plural) or *church* (singular)? Jesus said that He would build His *church* (singular). Yet, today there are many different churches. Many of them have names that are different from each other. They also differ in what they believe about various moral issues, in what they teach about how to become a Christian, in what they believe regarding how to organize the church, and in what they teach about how to worship God.

If you were to examine a directory of churches in your area, you would come to realize that there are numerous divergent names, and types, of churches. You also would recognize that among those who claim to be Christians, there is much division. Do you think this is pleasing to God? Is it acceptable to God for there to be so many different churches, with so many different names, teaching so many different things, and creating so much division?

Should the church that Jesus built tolerate such division? Is it acceptable to divide the "one body" of Christ in order to establish manmade churches or denominations? Should Christians separate themselves by different names, doctrines, or creeds? Ask yourself the following questions:

Should the body of Christ be divided?
Should the church have a multiplicity of names?
Should the church have a multiplicity of creeds?
Should the church teach doctrines not found in the Bible?

In the next section, let us seek to answer those questions, and, in particular, the question, "Must the church be unified?"

THE CHURCH IS ESSENTIAL AND IMPORTANT:

- **For salvation**
- **As an example of God's wisdom**
- **Within God's eternal purpose**
- **Because Christ loves the church**
- **Because only one exists**

About the Church

SECTION REVIEW: *IS THE CHURCH ESSENTIAL AND IMPORTANT?*

Answers to the following questions can be found in the section above.

STUDY QUESTIONS

1. According to Ephesians 3:8-11 and the verses below, is it possible for a person to please God by trying to "have an individual relationship with Jesus," but have no involvement in the church? YES / NO

   And He put all things under His feet, and gave Him to be head over all things to the church, which is His body, the fullness of Him who fills all in all (Ephesians 1:22-23).

   For He Himself is our peace, who has made both one, and has broken down the middle wall of separation, having abolished in His flesh the enmity, that is, the law of commandments contained in ordinances, so as to create in Himself one new man from the two, thus making peace, and that He might reconcile them both to God in one body through the cross, thereby putting to death the enmity (Ephesians 2:14-16).

2. According to Ephesians 2:16, are sinful humans reconciled to God (brought back together after being separated) in Christ's body, the church? YES / NO

3. According to Ephesians 3:8-11, Paul writes, "to the intent that now the manifold wisdom of God might be made known by the _____

   to the principalities and powers in the heavenly places, according to the _____ _____ which He accomplished in Christ Jesus our Lord."

4. Is it acceptable to God for racism or bigotry to exist within Christ's church? YES / NO

5. Does the Bible teach that the church was planned by Deity, prophesied by the prophets, predicted by Jesus, and established by God? YES / NO

6. During the first century, the eternal plan of God was realized. The _____ of Christ was established.

7. According to Ephesians 5:23 and 25, does Christ love the church and is He the Savior of the body? YES / NO

8. According to Ephesians 1:22-23, "He put all things under His feet, and gave Him to be head over all things to the church, which is

   _____ _____."

9. Must one be in the church, the body of Christ, to be saved? YES / NO

10. According to Ephesians 4:4-5, is there more than one body (church)? YES / NO

11. According to Matthew 16:18, did Jesus say that He would build one church (singular) or many churches (plural)? _____ _____

12. According to Matthew 16:18 and Ephesians 4:4, is it acceptable to God for different denominations to exist? YES / NO

An ANSWER KEY for the STUDY QUESTIONS is provided in the back of the book.

DECISION POINTS

A. Is the church important and essential? YES / NO

B. Do you love the church as Christ loved the church? YES / NO

C. Do you believe that Christ established only one church, and that He is its Head? YES / NO

D. Are you a member of Christ's church, or a member of a manmade denomination?

TALKING POINTS

A. According to Ephesians 2:14, under the Old Law, a "wall of separation" existed between Jews and Gentiles. How did Christ break down that wall?

B. According to Daniel 2:44, the prophet Daniel foretold "a kingdom which shall never be destroyed," and that would "break in pieces and consume" all other kingdoms. What were those other kingdoms, and what was the "kingdom which shall never be destroyed" that accomplished what Daniel had prophesied?

MUST THE CHURCH BE UNIFIED?

In today's world, there is division among those professing to follow Jesus. The acceptance and toleration of this division are often rationalized on the basis of a concept known as "denominationalism." But what, exactly, is denominationalism?

> "Denominationalism" simply means to name something. When you separate yourself into any group, then you are "denominated." If you were to ask someone what kind of Christian he is, he might tell you, "I'm *this* particular kind of Christian." He is denominating what he is. What happened here is that denominationalism split Christianity into so many bodies that it's nearly impossible to name all of them. Someone has estimated that there are over 600 in this country alone that claim to be "Christians," yet name themselves differently because they are following different creeds, different doctrines, or different dogmas. To denominate is to split or break up the church that Jesus died for and paid for with His blood (Acts 20:28).
>
> Keith Mosher Sr.
> Bible Instructor and Minister

The concept of denominationalism—which refers to breaking off from the whole by subscribing to a particular name and set of doctrines—promotes division and sectarianism. Interestingly, the concept of denominationalism is nowhere mentioned in the Bible. In fact, even a hint of division based on manmade doctrines, or the names and notoriety of men, is condemned. Consider, for example, what was happening in the Lord's church at Corinth.

In Acts 18, Luke tells us that while Paul was on one of his missionary journeys, he helped to establish the church in the city of Corinth. According to the account in Acts, Paul spent eighteen months teaching the word of God, following the baptism of many of the Corinthians who had heard, believed, and obeyed the Gospel. From Corinth, Paul eventually made his way to Asia Minor, where he worked in establishing the church at Ephesus. While in Ephesus, Paul received word that there were some problems occurring in the body of Christ at Corinth. One of the problems had to do with a division among its members regarding individual preferences for specific preachers.

> *For it has been declared to me concerning you, my brethren, by those of Chloe's* household, *that there are contentions among you. Now I say this, that each of you says, "I am of Paul," or "I am of Apollos," or "I am of Cephas," or "I am of Christ" Is Christ divided? Was Paul crucified for you? Or were you baptized in the name of Paul? (1 Corinthians 1:11-13).*

When Paul heard of these problems, he wrote (by inspiration of the Holy Spirit) the book of First Corinthians. In that epistle, he *strongly* condemned the practice of division.

About the Church

Now I plead with you, brethren, by the name of our Lord Jesus Christ, that you all speak the same thing, and that there be no divisions among you, but that you be perfectly joined together in the same mind and in the same judgment (1 Corinthians 1:10).

Unfortunately, some in the church at Corinth had begun dividing over preferences for various preachers. After being baptized, some began to say, "I am of Paul," or "I am of Cephas," or "I am of Christ." Paul, however, denounced their division by asking three important questions: Is Christ divided? Was Paul crucified for you? Or were you baptized in the name of Paul? (1 Corinthians 1:13).

The answers to these questions are obvious. First, *Christ is not divided.* In Mark 3:22-26, Christ stressed the unified nature of His essence. Second, Paul had not been crucified for them. And third, they were not baptized in the name of Paul. According to Matthew 28:19, sinners are baptized in the name of Christ.

Based on these criteria, would these Christians in Corinth have been wrong in calling themselves "Paulites?" Would they have sinned by naming the church after Paul (the "church of Paul")? Yes, they would have been wrong. And yes, they would have sinned against God.

What if today there was a preacher in the church by the name of Alex Campbell, who was himself a dynamic and powerful preacher? Let's say that he was an eminent and well-educated Bible scholar who had helped to convert thousands to Christ. If we, in seeking to honor him, began wearing the religious name, "Campbellite," would that be acceptable to God? Not according to Paul's teachings in 1 Corinthians 1! In order for one to be able to call oneself a "Campbellite," three things would have to be true:

1. **Christ would have to be divided.**
2. **A person would have to be baptized "in the name of Alex Campbell."**
3. **Alex Campbell would have to be crucified for that person.**

By calling yourself a Campbellite, you would be dividing the body of Christ, and would bring glory to Alex Campbell instead of bringing glory to Christ. In 1 Corinthians 1:31, Paul said, "He who glories, let him glory in the Lord." Peter wrote: "If anyone suffers as a Christian, let him not be ashamed, but let him glorify God *in this name*" (1 Peter 4:16, *American Standard Version*). What did Peter mean when he said that we are to glorify God "in this name"? Which name? The answer, of course, is the name *Christ!*

If it is wrong to divide the body of Christ over a preference for preachers, would it not be just as wrong to divide the body of

Christ over manmade creeds and doctrines? Would it not be wrong to divide the body of Christ by adopting unauthorized religious names, either for ourselves or for the congregation of which we are a member?

> One church may not teach the same thing as another church, but according to denominationalism, they are both "the church of Christ." Scripture teaches us, however, that there is one body, one church, and that that church teaches the same thing uniformly. That is what we need to strive to do today—speak "as the oracles of God," and not differentiate or denominate ourselves into a number of different groups, all claiming to be from the one body.
>
> B. J. Clarke
> Minister

The *unity of the church* is emphasized repeatedly in the New Testament. Thus, *we must not be guilty of dividing the body of Christ!* In fact, Jesus Himself prayed for the unity of all believers:

I do not pray for these alone, but also for those who will believe in Me through their word; that they all may be one, as You, Father, are in Me, and I in You; that they also may be one in Us, that the world may believe that You sent Me (John 17:20-21).

Paul specifically instructed the church to maintain the unity of the Spirit in the bond of peace:

I, therefore, the prisoner of the Lord, beseech you to walk worthy of the calling with which you were called, with all lowliness and gentleness, with longsuffering, bearing with one another in love, endeavoring to keep the unity of the Spirit in the bond of peace. There is one body and one Spirit, just as you were called in one hope of your calling; one Lord, one faith, one baptism; one God and Father of all, who is above all, and through all, and in you all (Ephesians 4:1-6).

Notice not only that *unity is demanded,* but also that *division and sectarianism are condemned.* Such errors are classified as works of the flesh that must not be practiced or tolerated.

Now the works of the flesh are evident, which are: adultery, fornication, uncleanness, lewdness, idolatry, sorcery, hatred, contentions, jealousies, outbursts of wrath, selfish ambitions, dissensions, heresies, envy, murders, drunkenness, revelries, and the like; of which I tell you beforehand, just as I also told you in time past, that those who practice such things will not inherit the kingdom of God (Galatians 5:19-21).

Now I urge you, brethren, note those who cause divisions and offenses, contrary to the doctrine which you learned, and avoid them. For those who are such do not serve our Lord Jesus Christ, but their own belly, and by smooth words and flattering speech deceive the hearts of the simple (Romans 16:17-18).

Division is condemned, which is why Christians must work diligently to maintain unity in the body of Christ (Ephesians 4:1-6). To be perfectly joined together in the same mind and in the same judgment, each of us must be willing to give up anything that is not authorized in the Bible. Unity demands that we worship and live according to God's word—and God's word alone! To maintain the unity of the spirit and the bond of peace will necessitate that we have a "thus saith the Lord" for all that we do and say. Paul put it in these words: "And whatever you do in word or deed, do all in the name of the Lord Jesus, giving thanks to God the Father through Him" (Colossians 3:17).

SECTION REVIEW: *MUST THE CHURCH BE UNIFIED?*

Answers to the following questions can be found in the section above.

STUDY QUESTIONS

1. According to the verse below, Jesus purchased the church with His blood. Today, many different religious "denominations" exist. To denominate is to split or break up the church for which Jesus died, and that He purchased with His blood. Is this acceptable to God? YES / NO

    Therefore take heed to yourselves and to all the flock, among which the Holy Spirit has made you overseers, to shepherd the church of God which He purchased with His own blood (Acts 20:28).

2. Does the Bible authorize the concept of denominationalism? YES / NO

3. According to 1 Corinthians 1:10, the apostle wrote to the church at Corinth "that there be no _____ among you, but that you be perfectly _____ _____ in the same mind and in the same judgment."

4. According to 1 Corinthians 1:10-13, would it have been wrong for Christians to begin calling themselves Paulites (after the apostle Paul). YES / NO

5. According to the verse below, there is _____ _____ _____ by which we must be saved.

    Nor is there salvation in any other, for there is no other name under heaven given among men by which we must be saved (Acts 4:12).

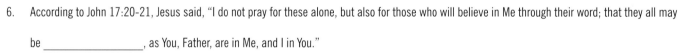

6. According to John 17:20-21, Jesus said, "I do not pray for these alone, but also for those who will believe in Me through their word; that they all may be _____, as You, Father, are in Me, and I in You."

7. According to Ephesians 4:1-6, did Paul stress the unity of Christians and the church? YES / NO

8. According to Galatians 5:19-21, are strife, division, parties, and factions in the church wrong? YES / NO

9. According to Colossians 3:17, is whatever we say or do to be done in the name of the Lord Jesus? YES / NO

An ANSWER KEY for the STUDY QUESTIONS is provided in the back of the book.

DECISION POINTS

A. If you are a member of a church that is *not* Christ's church, but is instead one of the many manmade divisions in religion today, are you *right* to remain in that church? YES / NO

B. According to Colossians 3:17, Paul wrote: "Whatever you do in word or deed, do all in the name of the Lord Jesus." Is the church of which you are a member obeying Paul's inspired command? YES / NO

TALKING POINTS

A. What is "sectarianism," and why is it condemned by God?

B. Why is it wrong to adopt a name for the church, or for individual Christians, which is not authorized by God in His word?

C. If it is wrong to call a Christian (or the church) a Paulite, what other religious names in existence today would not be acceptable?

CONCLUSION

To do something "in the name of the Lord Jesus" is to do it with His permission and approval. Ask yourself: Am I seeking the Lord's approval? Am I in His church? Am I wearing a religious name that brings glory to Christ? Am I living and worshiping in a way that is authorized by (and thus acceptable to) Christ? Am I striving to promote unity in the body of Christ by going to God's word and doing only those things that the Bible authorizes?

Would it not be wonderful if sincere truth seekers everywhere renounced the wearing of manmade religious names, abandoned their various creed books, "confessions of faith," and all unbiblical practices—and became *just* a member of the church of Christ revealed in the Bible? Such things would not only be "wonderful," but, in fact, we must make every effort to make it happen. So, in answering the question, "Must the church be unified?," we have to answer with a resounding "YES!"

Just as we have learned in this lesson that

the church is the body of Christ, and is composed of those who are the saved
and
the church is important, essential, and necessary,

so we also have learned that

the church must be unified.

These three truths are fundamental to The Faith. They are part of the blessed Gospel of Christ. They are part of the Truth—the word of God—which can set us free from the shackles of manmade religious names, doctrines, and practices. Will you accept and obey the truth about what the Bible teaches regarding Christ's church? You *can* know the truth, and the truth *will* set you free (John 8:32). I urge you to embrace the truth about the church as revealed within the pages of God's word.

CHAPTER REVIEW
Answers to the following questions can be found within this chapter.

STUDY QUESTIONS

1. According to Matthew 16:18, Jesus said, "On this rock I will build _____ church, and the gates of Hades shall not prevail against it."

2. According to Acts 2:41,46-47, "the Lord added to the church daily those who were being _____."

3. In 1 Corinthians 1:13, Paul asked: "Is Christ divided?" What is the correct answer? YES / NO

FOCUS QUESTIONS

1. According to Acts 2:47, God adds the saved to the church. Is it possible to be saved, yet *not* be in the church? YES / NO

2. According to Colossians 1:24, the church is Christ's body. According to Ephesians 4:4, there is only one body. Thus, how many churches did Christ establish? _____

3. This lesson discusses three different ways in which the word "church" is utilized in referring to the saved; one of the ways is *local*, as in "the church in Jerusalem" (Acts 11:22). What are the two other ways? (a) _____ (b) _____

An ANSWER KEY for the STUDY QUESTIONS and FOCUS QUESTIONS is provided in the back of the book.

THINGS YOU SHOULD KNOW

- The church is the body of Christ, and is composed of those who are saved.
- The church is important, essential, and necessary.
- The church must be unified.
- Jesus established the church; He is its Bridegroom; it is His bride; it must bear His name.
- The church is: the saved; the body of baptized believers; the body of Christ; the kingdom of God; the house of God; the temple of God.
- One must be in the church to be saved.
- Church division is sinful.

DIGGING DEEPER...

The material below is intended for those people who would like to study this subject further. It contains information that was not necessarily discussed in the lesson.

CHRIST AND THE CHURCH IN PROPHECY, PROMISE, AND FULFILLMENT

For unto us a Child is born, Unto us a Son is given; And the government will be upon His shoulder. And His name will be called Wonderful, Counselor, Mighty God, Everlasting Father, Prince of Peace. Of the increase of His government and peace There will be no end, Upon the throne of David and over His kingdom, To order it and establish it with judgment and justice From that time forward, even forever. The zeal of the Lord of hosts will perform this (Isaiah 9:6-7).

Therefore thus says the Lord GOD: "Behold, I lay in Zion a stone for a foundation, A tried stone, a precious cornerstone, a sure foundation; Whoever believes will not act hastily" (Isaiah 28:16).

And it shall come to pass afterward That I will pour out My Spirit on all flesh; Your sons and your daughters shall prophesy, Your old men shall dream dreams, Your young men shall see visions. And also on My menservants and on My maidservants I will pour out My Spirit in those days (Joel 2:28-29).

And He said to them, "Assuredly, I say to you that there are some standing here who will not taste death till they see the kingdom of God present with power" (Mark 9:1).

But Peter, standing up with the eleven, raised his voice and said to them, "Men of Judea and all who dwell in Jerusalem, let this be known to you, and heed my words. For these are not drunk, as you suppose, since it is only the third hour of the day. But this is what was spoken by the prophet Joel: 'And it shall come to pass in the last days, says God, That I will pour out of My Spirit on all flesh; Your sons and your daughters shall prophesy, Your young men shall see visions, Your old men shall dream dreams. And on My menservants and on My maidservants I will pour out My Spirit in those days; And they shall prophesy'" (Acts 2:14-18).

Praising God and having favor with all the people. And the Lord added to the church daily those who were being saved (Acts 2:47).

Knowing that you were not redeemed with corruptible things, like silver or gold, from your aimless conduct received by tradition from your fathers, but with the precious blood of Christ, as

About the Church

of a lamb without blemish and without spot. He indeed was fore-ordained before the foundation of the world, but was manifest in these last times for you (1 Peter 1:18-20).

Coming to Him as to a living stone, rejected indeed by men, but chosen by God and precious.... Therefore, to you who believe, He is precious; but to those who are disobedient, "The stone which the builders rejected Has become the chief cornerstone," (1 Peter 2:4,7).

THINGS TO THINK ABOUT...WHEN DIGGING DEEPER

1. Who was Isaiah prophesying of in Isaiah 9:6-7? _____

2. Who was the "precious corner stone" and "sure foundation" that Isaiah prophesied of in Isaiah 28:16? _____

3. In Mark 9:1, did Jesus teach that the kingdom of God (the church) would come in the lifetimes of those living in the first century? YES / NO

4. According to Acts 2:47, what important institution came into existence on the day of Pentecost after Jesus' resurrection?

   _____ _____

5. Do Joel 2:28-29 and Acts 2:14-18 teach that God was planning the church long before it began? YES / NO

6. "He indeed was _____ before the foundation of the world, but was _____ in these last times for you" (1 Peter 1:18-20).

7. Who was Peter referring to in 1 Peter 2:7 when he said, "the stone which the builders rejected has become the chief cornerstone?" _____

THE NEED FOR, REALITY OF, AND BLESSINGS FROM CHRIST AND THE CHURCH

Come to Me, all you who labor and are heavy laden, and I will give you rest. Take My yoke upon you and learn from Me, for I am gentle and lowly in heart, and you will find rest for your souls. For My yoke is easy and My burden is light (Matthew 11:28-30).

...Whoever desires to come after Me, let him deny himself, and take up his cross, and follow me (Mark 8:34).

Nor is there salvation in any other, for there is no other name under heaven given among men by which we must be saved (Acts 4:12).

Then Barnabas departed for Tarsus to seek Saul. And when he had found him, he brought him to Antioch. So it was that for a whole year they assembled with the church and taught a great many people. And the disciples were first called Christians in Antioch (Acts 11:25-26).

For all have sinned and fall short of the glory of God (Romans 3:23).

For the wages of sin is death, but the gift of God is eternal life in Christ Jesus our Lord (Romans 6:23).

Blessed be the God and Father of our Lord Jesus Christ, who hath blessed us with all spiritual blessings in heavenly places in Christ (Ephesians 1:3).

In Him we have redemption through His blood, the forgiveness of sins, according to the riches of His grace (Ephesians 1:7).

For the husband is head of the wife, as also Christ is head of the church; and He is the Savior of the body (Ephesians 5:23).

Therefore I endure all things for the sake of the elect, that they also may obtain the salvation which is in Christ Jesus with eternal glory (2 Timothy 2:10).

Do not fear any of those things which you are about to suffer. Indeed, the devil is about to throw some of you into prison, that you may be tested, and you will have tribulation ten days. Be faithful until death, and I will give you the crown of life (Revelation 2:10).

And they sang a new song, saying: "You are worthy to take the scroll, And to open its seals; For You were slain, And have redeemed us to God by Your blood Out of every tribe and tongue and people and nation" (Revelation 5:9).

THINGS TO THINK ABOUT…WHEN DIGGING DEEPER

8. According to Matthew 11:28-30, if we come to Jesus, He will give us _____.

9. Does Mark 8:34 teach that to come to Jesus we must deny ourselves, take up our crosses, and follow Him? YES / NO

10. Does Acts 4:12 teach that there are many different names we need in order to be saved? YES / NO

11. According to Acts 11:26, the members of the church, the disciples, were called _____.

12. "For the wages of sin is _____, but the gift of God is _____ _____ in Christ Jesus our Lord" (Romans 6:23).

13. According to Ephesians 1:3 and 7 and 2 Timothy 2:10, all spiritual blessings, redemption, forgiveness, and salvation are found only in _____.

14. According to Ephesians 5:23, will Christ save me if I am not part of His church? YES / NO

15. In Revelation 2:10, Jesus states that if we are faithful, He will give us the _____ _____ _____.

An ANSWER KEY for the DIGGING DEEPER QUESTIONS is provided in the back of the book.

Searching for Truth

ABOUT THE HOUSE OF GOD

Most people in the world live in some kind of house or dwelling. Those houses come in all shapes and sizes—with different floor plans and layouts, and furnished in a lot of different ways. Yet each home is precious and unique to its owner. But have you ever wondered whether or not God owns a house? And if He does, how could we recognize that house if we were to go in search of it today?

INTRODUCTION

Inspired by the Holy Spirit, the apostle Paul wrote the following to a young evangelist by the name of Timothy:

> *These things I write to you, though I hope to come to you shortly; but if I am delayed,* I write *so that you may know how you ought to conduct yourself in the house of God, which is the church of the living God, the pillar and ground of the truth (1 Timothy 3:14-15).*

From this passage, we learn that God has a house—a dwelling place. That house is known as "the church." The church, as we learned in the previous lesson, is composed of "the saved" of Christ. As "the saved," they are identified as the body, the kingdom, the temple of God, and, as we have just seen, the house of God.

God, as the Sovereign Power of the Universe, inhabits the entire Earth. He truly knows all, sees all, and is everywhere at all times. Yet there also is a sense in which God dwells in a very special way within the confines of His people, the church.

The church *building* is not *the church*. Rather, that building is merely a place where members of God's house meet on occasion to worship and study. According to 1 Corinthians 3:16, the church—as the dwelling place of God—*is* known as the house or temple of God. That house, as you might expect, is unique. It had a unique Architect and Builder. It had in the past, and still has today, a unique organizational structure and purpose. It also has several distinguishing traits and characteristics which, if we were to go in search of today, would enable us to properly identify its existence.

Let's search for that house. Let's search for the truth about the house of God. As we do, we need to ask three important questions:

1. **Who built the house of God?**
2. **What are the unique characteristics of the house of God?**
3. **Can we establish the house of God today?**

Let us begin by searching for an answer to the first question: "Who built the house of God?"

WHO BUILT THE HOUSE OF GOD?

It should not take us long to answer this question. In fact, you probably already know the answer. But in order to be sure, let us read the words of Jesus to discover for ourselves what He wants us to know about His church.

> *When Jesus came into the region of Caesarea Philippi, He asked His disciples, saying, "Who do men say that I, the Son of Man, am?" So they said, "Some say John the Baptist, some Elijah, and others Jeremiah or one of the prophets." He said to them, "But who do you say that I am?" Simon Peter answered and said, "You are the Christ, the Son of the living God." Jesus answered and said to him, "Blessed are you, Simon Bar-Jonah, for flesh and blood has not revealed* this *to you, but My Father who is in heaven. And I also say to you that you are Peter, and on this rock I will build My church, and the gates of Hades shall not prevail against it" (Matthew 16:13-18).*

In verse 18 of this passage, we can see quite clearly that Jesus is the Builder of the church. We might also notice that He is the *Owner* of His church, as is emphasized in His statement, "I will build *My* church." The possessive pronoun "My" clearly points to Jesus. So, He is both the Builder and the Owner of His church.

Read what the writer of the Book of Hebrews said on this subject, and notice Who is "over" (or "in charge of") the house of God:

> *Therefore, holy brethren, partakers of the heavenly calling, consider the Apostle and High Priest of our confession, Christ Jesus, who was faithful to Him who appointed Him, as Moses also* was faithful *in all His house. For this One has been counted worthy of more glory than Moses, inasmuch as He who built the house has more honor than the house. For every house is built by someone, but He who built all things* is God. *And Moses indeed* was faithful *in all His house as a servant, for a testimony of those things which would be spoken* afterward, *but Christ as a Son over His own house, whose house we are if we hold fast the confidence and the rejoicing of the hope firm to the end (Hebrews 3:1-6).*

About the House of God

From this passage (and from the information we learned in the previous lesson about the church) we can conclude that:

- **Jesus Christ, as God, has built a house.**
- **Christians (the saved) are that house.**
- **Jesus is over His house.**

So, yes, it is true that Christ is the Builder and the Owner of His house, the church. And He is over His church. But to what does the phrase "over His house" refer?

> The phrase "over His house" refers to the superiority of the Church Age over the old Mosaic Age. Back in that day and age, Moses, *as a servant,* was the head of that house. But Jesus, as the Christ, as the Son of God, and as the Heir, is the *Ruler* over *His* house, the church. The apostle Paul wrote, "And He is before all things, and in Him all things consist. And He is the head of the body, the church, who is the beginning, the firstborn from the dead, that in all things He may have the preeminence" (Colossians 1:17-18). Notice that the passage states that Jesus alone has this authority. No man, no body of men, and no council has this authority. It's that simple.
>
> Chuck Horner
> Bible Instructor and Minister

According to Colossians 1:17-18, Christ is the Head of the church. This means that He and He alone has the right to make rules and establish laws in regard to its nature, its worship, its organization, its work, and so on. No man, therefore, can claim the title "head of the church," since Jesus alone is the Head. Furthermore, no person should presume to claim ownership of the church built by Jesus, since Jesus is its Owner, Builder, and Head.

Christ is indeed "over" His house. But how *much* authority does Christ have? Jesus said, "*All* authority has been given to Me in heaven and on earth" (Matthew 28:18).

How much authority does Jesus have? He has *all* authority. That does not leave room for anyone else. *All* means *all.* If I want to know something about the house of God (the church), then I need to go to Jesus and Jesus alone, since He is the Builder and Owner of the church.

But now let us ask, "Since Christ is the Builder, Owner, and Head of His house, do you or I have the right to make modifications and/or additions to *His* house? Can we take it upon ourselves to change or remodel the house that Jesus has already built?"

Suppose you wanted to build a house in which to live. Suppose you possessed enough money to acquire the land and the materials, and that you decided to build the house with your own hands. Suppose, further, that you hired workers to aid you in constructing your house. You then commissioned them to build the house according to your specifications—with exactly the number of rooms requested, precisely the amount of floor space required, etc. Suppose that after your home was completed, you invited some friends or relatives to stay in your house. Would those friends or relatives have the right to modify *your* home to *their* liking? Could they begin to make changes in your house without your authorization? What if one day you discovered that your friends or relatives had done that very thing, and had taken it upon themselves to begin remodeling by adding a wall here, or a door there? How would you feel? Would that be acceptable? Absolutely not! Why not? Because the house belongs to *you! You* built it with your own hands and with your own money. Therefore, you and you alone possess the exclusive right to determine not only the design and layout, but also how the house will be maintained.

In a similar fashion, Christ, as the Builder of His house (the church), purchased with His own blood the people who make up the church (Acts 20:28; 1 Peter 1:18-19). He then commissioned the apostles to lay the foundation of the church, and to aid Him in constructing it according to its divine specifications (Ephesians 2:19-22; 1 Corinthians 3:10-11). As residents who are living in a house owned and built by Jesus, do *we* have the authority to remodel or modify things to *our* liking? Do we have the right to organize *His* house according to *our* own opinions, or to put a different name on the house, even though it does not belong to us? No. All of us surely recognize that as a resident, we must leave the house exactly as we found it, and must live in the house according to the divine principles found within the word of God. We have neither the right nor the authority to alter the specifications that are provided in the Bible.

Who, then, is the builder of *God's* house? *Jesus* is the Builder—and as the Builder and Owner, He has all authority over His house.

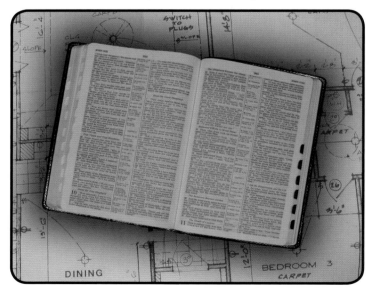

SECTION REVIEW: *WHO BUILT THE HOUSE OF GOD?*

Answers to the following questions can be found in the section above.

STUDY QUESTIONS

1. According to 1 Timothy 3:14-15, "the house of God" is the same as "the _____ of the living God."

2. Does the New Testament teach that phrases such as "the body," "the kingdom," "the saved," "the temple of God," and the "house of God" all refer to the church? YES / NO

3. According to Matthew 16:13-18:

   a. Who built the church? _____

   b. To Whom does the church belong? _____

4. According to Colossians 1:17-18, Jesus is "before all things, and in Him all things consist. And He is the _____ of the body, the

   church, who is the beginning, the firstborn from the dead, that in _____ things He may have the preeminence."

5. According to Matthew 28:18, Jesus has _____ authority in _____ and on _____.

6. According to the verses below, did Jesus (as God) purchase the church with His own blood? YES / NO

   Therefore take heed to yourselves and to all the flock, among which the Holy Spirit has made you overseers, to shepherd the church of God which He purchased with His own blood (Acts 20:28).

   Knowing that you were not redeemed with corruptible things, like *silver or gold, from your aimless conduct* received *by tradition from your fathers, but with the precious blood of Christ, as of a lamb without blemish and without spot (1 Peter 1:18-19).*

7. Since Christ purchased the church, and is both the builder and head of His house (the church), do you or I have the right to make modifications and/or additions to His house? YES / NO

8. According to the verses below, is the church built upon the foundation of the apostles with Christ Jesus Himself being the chief cornerstone? YES / NO

   Now, therefore, you are no longer strangers and foreigners, but fellow citizens with the saints and members of the household of God, having been built on the foundation of the apostles and prophets, Jesus Christ Himself being the chief cornerstone, in whom the whole building, being fitted together, grows into a holy temple in the Lord, in whom you also are being built together for a dwelling place of God in the Spirit (Ephesians 2:19-22).

9. Must the residents (Christians) of God's house (the church) live in that house according to the divine principles found within the word of God? YES / NO

An ANSWER KEY for the STUDY QUESTIONS is provided in the back of the book.

DECISION POINTS

A. Do you agree that Christ has *all* authority to make *all* decisions regarding His house, the church, and that humans do not have the right to either change or ignore Christ's decisions? YES / NO

B. Are you a member of the church described in the Bible, which Christ bought with His blood? YES / NO

TALKING POINTS

A. What does it mean for Christ to be "a Son over His own house" (Hebrews 3:6)?

B. What is the difference between Moses *as a servant* and Christ *as a Son?*

C. What role did the apostles have in building the house of God?

About the House of God

WHAT ARE THE UNIQUE CHARACTERISTICS OF THE HOUSE OF GOD?

As we examine the Bible, what will we discover about the design and construction of the house of God? How is it organized? How do its members worship? What doctrine is taught in God's house? And what name (or names) is (are) used in identifying God's house?

Every religious group (or "religious house") will have certain characteristics that distinguish it from every other religious group. Just as you can distinguish your house from other houses, the Lord's house can be distinguished from other would-be houses by its unique characteristics. Let us go on a search for the house of God. As we do, I ask you to think about the church you now attend. Does it look like the house of God as revealed in the New Testament?

Christ the Foundation
First, just like a house in which you or I might live today, the Lord's house, the church, has *a Foundation.*

> *...No other foundation can anyone lay than that which is laid, which is Jesus Christ (1 Corinthians 3:11; cf. Ephesians 2:19-22).*

The house of God must be built on Jesus Christ, not on the reputation of a man, or on human doctrines, creeds, or academic institutions. It never should be built on what may or may not be "culturally acceptable" or "politically correct." Rather, it must be built upon Jesus Christ, the One Who is "the same yesterday, today, and forever" (Hebrews 13:8). Is the church of which *you* are a member founded on Jesus?

Christ the Builder
Second, as we learned earlier, the Lord's house has *a Builder.*

> *...I will build My church, and the gates of Hades shall not prevail against it (Matthew 16:18).*

Who is the builder of the church you attend? Do you belong to the church built and established by Jesus?

Christ the Name
Third, another identifying mark of the Lord's house is its *name.* The church is referred to as *the church of God* (Acts 20:28; 1 Corinthians 1:2; Galatians 1:13; 1 Timothy 3:5). But because Christ *is* God (John 20:27-28), it also is referred to as *the church of Christ* (Romans 16:16—"the churches of Christ greet you"). Naming the church *for* Christ brings glory to the One Who purchased it. In Acts 20:28, the apostle Paul said that Christ purchased the church "with His own blood."

Suppose you were purchasing a piece of real estate. And suppose you were providing all of the funds necessary for the purchase of the property. Whose name would you want on the title of ownership or deed? Why, *your* name, of course! *You* bought it, and *you* own it. Therefore, *your name* ought to be on the deed. In the very same way, because Christ purchased the church, shouldn't *His* name be on the title of ownership? Indeed it should! It belongs to Christ, and it ought to bear His name, not the name of some other person or group.

Consider also that the church is referred to in the New Testament as "the bride of Christ" (Ephesians 5: 22-33; Romans 7:1-4; 2 Corinthians 11:2). What husband (including Christ as the church's Bridegroom) would want *his* bride to wear the name of *some other man?* Should not the *bride* of Christ wear the *name* of Christ? In New Testament times, the church did this very thing. It bore the name of the One Who died for its members.

> *Greet one another with a holy kiss. The churches of Christ greet you (Romans 16:16).*

So, yes, the house of God has a unique Foundation, Builder and name. Does the church *you* attend wear the name of Christ?

Christ the Organizer
Fourth, another characteristic of both a house and a church is *its organization.* In the Lord's house, Christ "is the head of the church" (Colossians 1:18). In this passage, the word "church" is used in a *universal* sense. In the New Testament, we also read of that body being spoken of in a *local* sense, such as "the church at Corinth," "the church at Ephesus," or "the church at Philippi." Once established, these churches were organized under the leadership and direction of men called elders, who were to shepherd and guide each congregation or body of God's people.

> *So when they had appointed elders in every church, and prayed with fasting, they commended them to the Lord in whom they had believed (Acts 14:23).*

When we talk about the scriptural organization of the church of Christ, we need to understand that the churches of Christ (Romans 16:16) are local congregations. Those who are members of those congregations are part of the body of Christ universal, over which He is the Head, and over which He has authority. Christ has given instructions regarding the organization of each local church. There are to be men, known as elders, who oversee that local work.

Bobby Liddell
Bible Instructor and Minister

The term "elder" refers to someone who, along with other elders in a given congregation, was responsible for shepherding a single congregational flock. In the language of the New Testament, these men were identified by three different Greek words. Each of these words is used interchangeably, and can be found in such passages as 1 Peter 5:1 and Acts 20:17,28. They are translated by six English words.

Presbuteros	**Elder or Presbyter**
Episkopos	**Bishop or Overseer**
Poimen	**Pastor or Shepherd**

All of these terms refer to the same individuals—individuals who had met the qualifications as outlined in 1 Timothy 3:1-7 and Titus 1:7-9. In those passages, we learn that an elder had to meet certain qualifications, such as being hospitable, just, holy, etc. Here is what is required to become an elder:

A bishop then must be blameless, the husband of one wife, temperate, sober-minded, of good behavior, hospitable, able to teach; not given to wine, not violent, not greedy for money, but gentle, not quarrelsome, not covetous; one who rules his own house well, having his children in submission with all reverence (1 Timothy 3:2-4).

Not only did these men have to meet these qualifications, but we also learn from reading the New Testament that these bishops or elders were charged with the exclusive responsibility of shepherding the single flock of which they were a part. The apostle Peter, who himself was an elder, explained the work and limits of an elder's oversight when he wrote:

The elders who are among you I exhort, I who am a fellow elder and a witness of the sufferings of Christ, and also a partaker of the glory that will be revealed: Shepherd the flock of God which is among you, serving as overseers, not by compulsion but willingly, not for dishonest gain but eagerly (1 Peter 5:1-2).

There is absolutely no evidence or authorization in the Bible for a group of elders or a single bishop to exercise authority outside the local congregation. Thus, the church at Philippi did not have elders who could oversee the affairs of the congregation at Ephesus, or vice versa. There was no hierarchal structure in the church, other than Christ as the Head. The prophets and apostles helped lay the foundation. In the New Testament, congregations were organized under an eldership, with each eldership overseeing the work of their own flock.

For a church of Christ to be scripturally organized, it needs to be by the pattern of the Holy Scriptures. In the New Testament, we see churches with *a plurality* of elders (Acts 14:23) over *one* congregation, which they tended (1 Peter 5:2ff.). There is wisdom in God's plan, because He made sure that with a plurality of el-

ders, if one man became morally or doctrinally contaminated, it would not necessarily contaminate the whole leadership. There is a system of checks and balances that God has built into this. There were deacons in the New Testament, but not a "board of deacons," per se. Deacons in the New Testament served under men who were elders—men who had to meet certain qualifications, according to 1 Timothy 3:1-7. Deacons, too, had to meet certain qualifications, as found in 1 Timothy 3:8-13. Preachers were never overseers of the church in the first century. In God's pattern, preachers are to serve under the oversight of elders. They are not the leaders of the church, in the sense that they make the final decisions. Philippians 1 talks about the bishops [elders and bishops are interchangeable terms] and the deacons. Thus, you have elders overseeing a local flock, with deacons serving under their authority. Preachers and members do the same thing, and follow the oversight of the elders who rule over them (Hebrews 13:17). That is God's plan, and it is one that we need to follow.

B. J. Clarke

Minister

God's house has a Foundation, a Builder, a name, and a unique organization. Is the religious house of which you are a part organized according to the Lord's specifications?

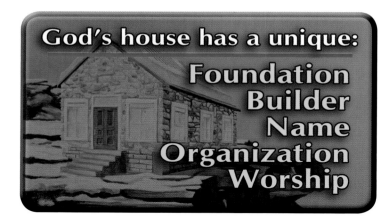

Now, let us notice that it also has *a unique form of worship.*

Christ the Ordainer of Acceptable Worship

Fifth, as directed by Jesus, true worshippers are to worship God "in spirit and in truth."

> *God is Spirit, and those who worship Him must worship in spirit and truth (John 4:24).*

Jesus said that we must worship God in truth. As we learned in lesson two, "the truth" is the same thing as "the word of God." Therefore, to worship God "in truth" is to worship Him according to His word. According to that word, it *is* possible to worship God *in vain.* Jesus taught that worship becomes vain when the com-

mandments of men are taught in the place of what is doctrinally sound or true.

> *And in vain they worship Me, Teaching as doctrines the commandments of men (Matthew 15:9).*

Thus, we see that in God's house, not just any kind of worship is acceptable to Him. Rather, our worship must be *authorized* by God. What, then, are the elements of acceptable worship? In the first century, how did Christians worship? And how should Christians today worship?

When Christians Assemble, They...

Pray

According to the Bible, when Christians come together in an assembly to worship, they pray (Acts 2:42; 4:31; 1 Timothy 2:1-6; 1 Thessalonians 5:17; Acts 12:5). They pray through ("in the name of") Jesus as the only true Mediator between God and man. Prayer was a very important part of the worship of the church during the first century, and it still is today.

But Christians, as a part of their worship, also must:

Proclaim the Word of God

When the members of God's house come together, the word of God is preached (Acts 20:7,20; 1 Corinthians 14). Preaching is designed for instruction and edification. It is designed to nurture and strengthen the residents of God's glorious kingdom, as well as to convert the lost to Jesus. The teaching of God's word is an essential ingredient in the life and work of the church. It is the source of the food that Christians need to maintain their spiritual strength.

But let us also notice that in the Lord's house, Christians:

Contribute to a Common Treasury (upon the first day of each week)

When the church was established in the first century, there arose an immediate need to finance the work of the church. There were widows who needed financial assistance, preachers who needed support, and families that were destitute. In response to this, the congregations reached out to help, frequently doing so by means of a free-will offering collected from the members *each* first day of the week (1 Corinthians 16:1-2; 2 Corinthians 9:6-7). Under the Old Testament, Jews were required to give a tenth of what they earned or produced (known as "tithing"). But in God's new house, the church, no such tithing requirement is imposed. Instead, Christians are called upon to give as God has prospered them, and to do so with cheerful hearts:

> *But this I say: He who sows sparingly will also reap sparingly, and he who sows bountifully will also reap bounti-*

fully. So let *each one* give *as he purposes in his heart, not grudgingly or of necessity; for God loves a cheerful giver (2 Corinthians 9:6-7).*

In addition to giving each first day of the week, those in God's house:

Partake of the Lord's Supper (on the first day of each week)

The first day of the week is a very important day in the life of the church, for it was on this day that the church was established. It was on this day that Jesus was resurrected from the dead. And, it was on this day that the church of the New Testament met to partake of the Lord's Supper (Acts 20:7; Matthew 26:26-28; Acts 2:42). The Lord's Supper is a special memorial meal that calls to remembrance the body and blood of Jesus. Not only does the meal remind Christians of what Christ has done for them, but it also serves as a testimony to the non-Christian about the love of Christ for sinners. Just as singing, giving, preaching, and praying do not become commonplace (even though they are done every week), the Lord's Supper does not lose its significance when it is celebrated each week either. In the first century, the Lord's Supper was a central part of the church's worship, and its weekly observance continues to be an identifying mark of the Lord's house today.

Finally, when the house of God assembles for worship, the members:

Praise God and Edify One Another through Singing

Let the word of Christ dwell in you richly in all wisdom, teaching and admonishing one another in psalms and hymns and spiritual songs, singing with grace in your hearts to the Lord (Colossians 3:16; cf. Ephesians 5:19; 1 Corinthians 14:15).

Music is an important part of the worship of the church. Yet, the music of the New Testament church was quite different from that which frequently is encountered among denominations today. The music found in God's house is *a cappella,* which is to say that it is singing without the accompaniment of any type of musical instrument.

> When it comes to deciding what we do in worship, what the plan of salvation is, or how the church is to be organized, those types of issues have to be determined, not by popular vote of uninspired men, but by asking, "What did Jesus say about this through His apostles and through His own words during His earthly ministry?" Therefore, now that we know what He said, are we willing to accept His authority and to do exactly what He says for us to do, in exactly the way He says for us to do it?
>
> B. J. Clarke
> Minister

> Instrumental music was not introduced until the seventh century A.D. There is no indication in the writings of the so-called "church fathers" in the first three or four centuries of the existence of the church of instrumental music ever being introduced into Christian worship. There may have been a few individuals who talked about it, but the use of instrumental music in worship to God was never an accepted practice during the first four or five centuries of the church's existence. In the 900s, it finally was brought in as an accepted part of Christian worship. It so divided the church at that time that the Eastern Orthodox Church never could accept it, and does not accept it even today. When the Protestant Reformation came along in the 1500s, even among some of the greatest reformers (such as John Calvin, John Wesley, and Martin Luther) there was aggressive opposition to the use of instrumental music in worship.
>
> Ben Moseley
> University Professor and Minister

When the use of mechanical instruments was gradually introduced into the worship services of various denominations, there were some prominent preachers among those denominations who opposed its use.

> Music, as a science, I esteem and admire. But instruments of music in the house of God I abominate and abhor. This is the abuse of music; and here I register my protest against all such corruptions in the worship of the Author of Christianity (Adam Clarke, *Adam Clarke's Commentary,* on Amos 6:5).

> I have no objections to instruments of music in our chapels, providing they are neither heard nor seen (John Wesley, as quoted in *Adam Clarke's Commentary,* on Amos 6:5).

While the fact that various Bible scholars of the past deplored the use of mechanical instruments in worship is certainly noteworthy,

About the House of God

it is of far greater importance to point out that the New Testament nowhere authorizes their use today.

The New Testament commandments for Christians to sing praises to God *never* mention mechanical instruments. In fact, according to *Bauer's Greek Dictionary*, the use of the word *psallo*—translated as "psalms" in Ephesians 5:19—means "'sing,' *exclusively*."

When God said that we are "to sing," that commandment excluded all other types of music.

> The reason we do not use instrumental music is because it is not authorized. People will often say, "But it doesn't say *not* to." That has nothing to do with it. Suppose you get up in the morning, you feel bad, and so you go to the doctor. The doctor says that you have a virus, and writes you a prescription that calls for sulfur. You take it to the pharmacist, the pharmacist looks at it, and says to himself, "This calls for sulfur. But I'll add a little penicillin, too." Later, you learn about what the pharmacist did, and you return to ask him, "Why did you do that?" He says, "Well, it didn't say *not* to." That has nothing to do with it. All he had the right to do was to give you what the doctor prescribed. The only way for us to know what pleases God is to ask, "What does His word say?" *Every* verse in the New Testament dealing with music in worship, or the kind of music God wants, refers to vocal music. Thus, that is what is authorized, and nothing else is. For example, when God told Noah to make the ark, He did not say, "Don't use hickory" or "Don't use walnut." When God told Noah to use gopher wood, that excluded every other kind of wood.
>
> James Meadows
> Bible Instructor and Minister

The singing that is unique to God's house is most assuredly *a cappella* (without the accompaniment of mechanical instruments). But what about *before* the establishment of the Lord's church? Aren't musical instruments mentioned in the Old Testament?

> Yes, they are, but the Old Testament reflected a very elementary scheme of things, a carnal system (see Heb. 9:10). The Old Testament contained the offerings of bloody sacrifices. The Old Testament had the burning of incense. The Old Testament had a physical, tribal priesthood through whom the rank and file of the people approached God. But that carnal system was laid aside, as the writer of Hebrews argues, in chapter nine of that document. The Old Testament regime was superseded by a spiritual system.
>
> It behooves, then, the truth-seeker of today not to go beyond what is written in the word of God. As God has specified the elements of the fruit of the vine and bread to be utilized in the Lord's Memorial Supper, so He has specified singing as opposed to playing an instrument. I am sure that none of us would add rice or Coca-Cola® to the Lord's Supper, even though we might like them, and even though God has not specifically condemned them. Well,

> what about adding rice, Coca-Cola®, and mechanical instruments to the worship? Would this be acceptable? Christians of the first century had instruments of music at their disposal, but they chose not to use them as a part of their worship. It was a distinguishing characteristic of the Lord's church.
>
> Ben Moseley
> University Professor and Minister

Does the church you attend have this distinguishing characteristic? Does the church you attend worship according to the Bible? The distinguishing marks of *a cappella* music, and the other unique forms of worship (along with the unique foundation, organization, name, Founder, and Builder), are all essential parts of what make up the New Testament house of God. These characteristics and unique traits are but a few of the examples found in the New Testament that reveal the peculiar nature of the Lord's church. Other distinguishing traits of the house of God would include:

Its Doctrine (The Word of God)
The unique doctrine of the house of God (the church) is the Bible, the word of God (2 Timothy 3:16-17).

Its Work (Evangelism, Edification, Benevolence)
As the house of God, the church also includes a narrow scope of work (Matthew 28:18-20; 1 Corinthians 16:1-2) involving evangelism, edification of its members, and benevolence (helping those who are in need).

Its Membership
The house of God also has a unique membership composed of people who are dedicated to being disciples of Christ (Acts 6:7), and who simply wear the name "Christian" (Acts 11:26; 1 Peter 4:16). Many of the religious names worn today were not in existence during the first century. Instead, baptized believers in the Bible wore the name of the One Who gave His life on Calvary—Christ.

Its Priesthood
A study of the New Testament reveals that each individual Christian is a part of the priesthood (1 Peter 2:9; Revelation 1:5-6; cf. Galatians 3:27). According to the Bible, a clergy/laity system should not exist. In God's sight, *every* baptized believer is considered a priest, and therefore is able (and is expected) to minister within the house/temple of God.

Its Ministers
Finally, the Lord's house contains ministers such as deacons and preachers (or evangelists) who are required to meet certain qualifications as outlined in 1 Timothy 3:8-13 and 2 Timothy 4:5. These men are simply servants in the body of Christ who, along with all members of the church, are prohibited from wearing religious titles such as "father" or "reverend."

Do not call anyone on earth your father; for One is your Father, He who is in heaven (Matthew 23:9).

He sent redemption unto his people: he hath commanded his covenant for ever: holy and reverend is his name (Psalm 111:9, King James Version*).*

In answering our second major question, we can see clearly that God's house has many unique, distinguishing characteristics. With each characteristic, we can see how the church of Jesus Christ should be organized, the manner in which it should worship, and what it should teach.

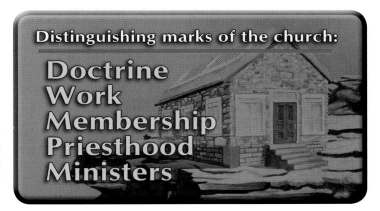

Distinguishing marks of the church:
Doctrine
Work
Membership
Priesthood
Ministers

SECTION REVIEW: *WHAT ARE THE UNIQUE CHARACTERISTICS OF THE HOUSE OF GOD?*

Answers to the following questions can be found in the section above.

STUDY QUESTIONS

1. According to Hebrews 13:8, the house of God must be built upon Jesus Christ, the One Who is "the same yesterday, today, and _____."

2. According to Romans 16:16:

    a. Do you read of the church of Christ in the Bible? YES / NO

    b. Would it be wrong to call God's house (the church) by this name? YES / NO

    c. Would this name glorify the One who built the church and bought it with His own blood? YES / NO

3. According to Acts 14:23 and the verses below:

    a. What office or leadership role within the church is under discussion in these passages? _____

    b. Do the terms elder and bishop refer to the same office? YES / NO

    c. Must an elder be married? YES / NO

    d. Must an elder have children? YES / NO

    e. May a recent convert (novice) serve as an elder? YES / NO

    This is a faithful saying: If a man desires the position of a bishop, he desires a good work. A bishop then must be blameless, the husband of one wife, temperate, sober-minded, of good behavior, hospitable, able to teach; not given to wine, not violent, not greedy for money, but gentle, not quarrelsome, not covetous; one who rules his own house well, having his children in submission with all reverence (for if a man does not know how to rule his own house, how will he take care of the church of God?); not a novice, lest being puffed up with pride he fall into the same condemnation as the devil. Moreover he must have a good testimony among those who are outside, lest he fall into reproach and the snare of the devil (1 Timothy 3:1-7).

    For this reason I left you in Crete, that you should set in order the things that are lacking, and appoint elders in every city as I commanded you—if a man is blameless, the husband of one wife, having faithful children not accused of dissipation or insubordination. For a bishop must be blameless, as a steward of God, not self-willed, not quick-tempered, not given to wine, not violent, not greedy for money, but hospitable, a lover of what is good, sober-minded, just, holy, self-controlled, holding fast the faithful word as he has been taught, that he may be able, by sound doctrine, both to exhort and convict those who contradict (Titus 1:5-9).

About the House of God

4. According to Acts 14:23, 1 Peter 5:1, and the verses below, are terms like "elder," "presbyter," "shepherd," "bishop," "pastor," and "overseer" interchangeable terms that are used to describe the same office? YES / NO

    From Miletus he sent to Ephesus and called for the elders of the church (Acts 20:17).

    Therefore take heed to yourselves and to all the flock, among which the Holy Spirit has made you overseers, to shepherd the church of God which He purchased with His own blood (Acts 20:28).

5. Is there any biblical authority for a group of elders, or a single bishop, to exercise authority outside the *local* congregation? YES / NO

6. According to John 4:24, must we worship God according to truth? YES / NO

7. According to the verses below:

    a. What is truth? _____ _____

    b. Since we must worship God in truth (John 4:24), must we worship as God has directed in the Bible? YES / NO

    Jesus spoke these words, lifted up His eyes to heaven, and said: "Father,…Sanctify them by Your truth. Your word is truth" (John 17:1, 17).

8. According to Matthew 15:9, is it possible to worship God in vain? YES / NO

9. According to the verses below, when Christians assemble, they are to _____ to God.

    And they continued steadfastly in the apostles' doctrine and fellowship, in the breaking of bread, and in prayers (Acts 2:42).

    And when they had prayed, the place where they were assembled together was shaken; and they were all filled with the Holy Spirit, and they spoke the word of God with boldness (Acts 4:31).

10. According to the verses below, "Paul _____" to the disciples who had gathered to break bread upon the first day of the week.

    Now on the first day of the week, when the disciples came together to break bread, Paul, ready to depart the next day, spoke to them and continued his message until midnight (Acts 20:7).

11. According to 2 Corinthians 9:6-7 and the verses below, Christians are taught that when they assemble on the first day of the week, they are

    to_____ to a common treasury.

    Now concerning the collection for the saints, as I have given orders to the churches of Galatia, so you must do also: On the first day of the week let each one of you lay something aside, storing up as he may prosper, that there be no collections when I come (1 Corinthians 16:1-2).

12. According to Acts 20:7 and Acts 2:42, when Christians assemble on the first day of the week, they are to _____ _____ (i.e. partake of the Lord's Supper).

13. According to Colossians 3:16 and the verses below, when Christians assemble to worship, they are to _____ to God.

    Speaking to one another in psalms and hymns and spiritual songs, singing and making melody in your heart to the Lord (Ephesians 5:19).

    What is the conclusion then? I will pray with the spirit, and I will also pray with the understanding. I will sing with the spirit, and I will also sing with the understanding (1 Corinthians 14:15).

14. According to Colossians 3:16, Ephesians 5:19, and 1 Corinthians 14:15, do the Scriptures provide any authority for the use of instruments of music in worship to God? YES / NO

15. When God said that we are "to sing," that commandment excluded all other types of _____.

16. Would it be wrong to add rice, Coca-Cola®, and mechanical instruments to the worship of the church? YES / NO

17. According to the verses below, is every individual Christian a part of the priesthood? YES / NO

> *But you* are *a chosen generation, a royal priesthood, a holy nation, His own special people, that you may proclaim the praises of Him who called you out of darkness into His marvelous light (1 Peter 2:9).*

> *And from Jesus Christ, the faithful witness, the firstborn from the dead, and the ruler over the kings of the earth. To Him who loved us and washed us from our sins in His own blood, and has made us kings and priests to His God and Father, to Him* be *glory and dominion forever and ever. Amen (Revelation 1:5-6).*

An ANSWER KEY for the STUDY QUESTIONS is provided in the back of the book.

DECISION POINTS

A. Who is the builder of the church *you* attend? _____

B. Do *you* belong to the church built and established *by Jesus?* YES / NO

C. Can the unique characteristics of God's house, as mentioned in this section, be found in the church where you attend? YES / NO

D. If the church where you attend does not worship according to the Bible, would it be acceptable to continue your support of such a church? YES / NO

TALKING POINTS

A. According to 2 Timothy 3:16-17, the unique doctrine of the house of God (the church) is the Bible, the word of God. Is there any place in the church, then, for manmade creeds and doctrines?

B. According to 1 Peter 2:9, Revelation 1:5-6, and Galatians 3:27, each individual Christian is a part of the priesthood. Is there a place within Christ's church, then, for a clergy/laity system?

C. According to the verses below, the Bible regards the church as the bride of Christ. What implications does this have for the name of the church, and for the relationship it has with its bridegroom?

> *Wives, submit to your own husbands, as to the Lord. For the husband is head of the wife, as also Christ is head of the church; and He is the Savior of the body. Therefore, just as the church is subject to Christ, so* let *the wives* be *to their own husbands in everything. Husbands, love your wives, just as Christ also loved the church and gave Himself for her, that He might sanctify and cleanse her with the washing of water by the word, that He might present her to Himself a glorious church, not having spot or wrinkle or any such thing, but that she should be holy and without blemish. So husbands ought to love their own wives as their own bodies; he who loves his wife loves himself. For no one ever hated his own flesh, but nourishes and cherishes it, just as the Lord* does *the church. For we are members of His body, of His flesh and of His bones. "For this reason a man shall leave his father and mother and be joined to his wife, and the two shall become one flesh." This is a great mystery, but I speak concerning Christ and the church. Nevertheless let each one of you in particular so love his own wife as himself, and let the wife* see *that she respects* her *husband (Ephesians 5:22-33).*

> *Or do you not know, brethren (for I speak to those who know the law), that the law has dominion over a man as long as he lives? For the woman who has a husband is bound by the law to* her *husband as long as he lives. But if the husband dies, she is released from the law of* her *husband. So then if, while* her *husband lives, she marries another man, she will be called an adulteress; but if her husband dies, she is free from that law, so that she is no adulteress, though she has married another man. Therefore, my brethren, you also have become dead to the law through the body of Christ, that you may be married to another—to Him who was raised from the dead, that we should bear fruit to God (Romans 7:1-4).*

> *For I am jealous for you with godly jealousy. For I have betrothed you to one husband, that I may present* you as *a chaste virgin to Christ (2 Corinthians 11:2).*

CAN WE ESTABLISH THE HOUSE OF GOD TODAY?

Now, let us ask our third major question: "Can we establish this house today?" In other words, can the house that Jesus built and established in the first century—the church about which we read in the Bible—be established or built today in your community or neighborhood? Let us ask one who happens to be both a carpenter and a preacher.

> Churches are a lot like houses. Houses have a design, and therefore a designer. Houses have a foundation and structure. They have unique characteristics that make them peculiar to the individual homeowner. And, something else every house has is a set of blueprints. In building a house, I would not know where to begin without a set of blueprints or a plan. By following the blueprints, I can construct a house exactly as the designer or architect intended. But what is noteworthy is that if I was to take a set of blueprints, I could build the same house in North or South America, Australia, Africa, Europe, or Asia. As long as the building materials were still in existence I could build an identical house in any one of those places now, or fifty years from now, simply by following the blueprints.
>
> When it comes to building the Lord's house, I can do the same thing. I could take the Bible and use it as a pattern or blueprint, and build the same church in North or South America, Africa, or anywhere else. If I followed its instructions exactly in terms of its organization, its name, and its worship, and if I taught exactly what is revealed in the Bible regarding its terms of entrance and membership, would it not be the house of God? If I could take a denominational creed book, study it, and establish a denominational church through its by-laws, why couldn't I just read the New Testament of Christ and use it to establish a church of Christ? Indeed "Christ's church" and "God's house" are one and the same. If I want to establish God's house in any community, then I better follow the blueprint found in the New Testament.
>
> Thomas Moore
> Minister and House Builder

It certainly is true that the Bible should (and must!) be used as our blueprint for both the establishment of the church and for living the Christian life. Consider, for example, what the apostle Paul said about the word of God being a blueprint or pattern.

> *Hold fast the pattern of sound words which you have heard from me, in faith and love which are in Christ Jesus (2 Timothy 1:13).*

Read, too, what Paul had to say about following the traditions established by the apostles in the written word.

> *Therefore, brethren, stand fast and hold the traditions*

which you were taught, whether by word or our epistle (2 Thessalonians 2:15).

According to Ephesians 2:19-22, the divinely appointed apostles assisted Jesus in laying the foundation of the church. We learn from Matthew 16:19 that whatever they loosed or bound on Earth had (according to the force of the Greek terminology used in the passage) *already been bound or loosed* by God in Heaven. As the Lord's ambassadors (2 Corinthians 5:20), the apostles were establishing church precedence that all followers of Jesus are to follow. The apostles' commandments and practices are fully explained and detailed within the pages of the New Testament. The New Testament became the church's blueprint, and is a blueprint that we today are required to follow. If we want to maintain our fellowship in the body of Christ, then we must obey the traditions set forth by the apostles within the New Testament.

> *And if anyone does not obey our word in this epistle, note that person and do not keep company with him, that he may be ashamed (2 Thessalonians 3:14).*

Thus, in answering our third major question, "Can we build the house of God today?," we must answer unequivocally, "Yes!" In fact, not only *can* we build the house of God today, but more im-

portant, we *must* build that house according to the divine specifications as revealed in what the apostles wrote by means of the Holy Spirit. Following apostolic authority as revealed in the written word of the New Testament is not an *option*. What is written, therefore, *must* be followed and obeyed. And, according to Deuteronomy 4:2, we must not add to the word of God. That same warning is given in the New Testament as well.

For I testify to everyone who hears the words of the prophecy of this book: If anyone adds to these things, God will add to him the plagues that are written in this book; and if anyone takes away from the words of the book of this prophecy, God shall take away his part from the Book of Life, from the holy city, and from the things which are written in this book (Revelation 22:18-19).

SECTION REVIEW: *CAN WE ESTABLISH THE HOUSE OF GOD TODAY?*

Answers to the following questions can be found in the section above.

STUDY QUESTIONS

1. According to 2 Timothy 1:13 and 2 Thessalonians 2:15, is the Bible a blueprint or pattern for building the house of God? YES / NO

2. According to 2 Thessalonians 2:15 and 2 Thessalonians 3:14, the church must obey and "hold the _____" set forth by the apostles in the New Testament.

3. According to the verses below, since the apostles were Christ's ambassadors, and were given authority to establish church precedence that all followers of Jesus are to follow, Christians today must _____ the apostles' commandments and follow their practices as explained within the pages of the New Testament.

   Now then, we are ambassadors for Christ, as though God were pleading through us: we implore you on Christ's behalf, be reconciled to God (2 Corinthians 5:20).

   And I will give you the keys of the kingdom of heaven, and whatever you bind on earth will be bound in heaven, and whatever you loose on earth will be loosed in heaven (Matthew 16:19).

4. According to 2 Thessalonians 3:14, Christians should not _____ _____ with those people who do not obey the words of the apostles as found in their writings (or epistles).

5. Do we have enough information within the New Testament to build the house of God *today?* YES / NO

6. According to Revelation 22:18-19 and the verse below, we must neither _____ to nor _____ from the word of God.

   You shall not add to the word which I command you, nor take from it, that you may keep the commandments of the LORD your God which I command you (Deuteronomy 4:2).

An ANSWER KEY for the STUDY QUESTIONS is provided in the back of the book.

DECISION POINTS

A. Are you a member of the church that has been established according to the divine specifications as revealed in what the apostles wrote by means of the Holy Spirit? YES / NO

B. The New Testament provides a blueprint for building the Lord's church. Is the church of which you are a member built according to that divine blueprint? YES / NO

About the House of God

C. If not, are you willing to go in search of the Lord's house? YES / NO

D. If the church of Christ does not exist within your community, would you and/or others be willing to take the Bible, and the Bible alone, and establish it? YES / NO

TALKING POINTS

A. Explain why Christ's church should be the same all over the world.

B. According to 2 Timothy 1:13, Christians must "hold fast the pattern of sound words" found within the blueprint, the Bible. Explain what is likely to happen if Christians do not do this.

C. Have others throughout the last 2000 years attempted to change and/or modify the house of God? In what ways?

CONCLUSION

Now let us ask: Have you, or those with whom you worship, added something to the Lord's house that was never intended or authorized by God? Does the church where you attend possess the characteristics as revealed in the New Testament? If you were to make a comparison between the church of the New Testament and the church you attend, would you find it had been built on Jesus? Does the church to which you belong wear the name of Christ? Is Jesus the Head of the church where you attend? Is it organized with qualified elders and deacons? Does it worship in truth? And, finally, does the church where you now worship teach that there is only *one* church to which baptized believers are added? If not, then we plead with you, go today in search of a true church of Christ.

Thus far in our search for truth, we have seen that the Lord does indeed have a house, and that His house is the same as His church, the kingdom. We also have learned that Jesus is the Builder of that house, and that His house has numerous unique, identifying characteristics. We also have learned that in establishing God's house today, we must follow the blueprint as revealed in the New Testament, and that we must not deviate from its plan.

Are *you* a member of God's house? If you are, have you been guilty of altering the pattern in establishing God's house? The Lord has only *one* house. If the one true church exists within your community, then why not go search for it? If it does not exist, then we plead with you to go back to the Bible (which is the only source of truth for establishing that church), and begin today to restore the church as designed by Jesus.

In John 4:24, we learn that those who worship God *must* worship Him in Spirit and in truth. According to John 17:17, the word of God is truth. Are *you* worshipping God according to truth? Are you part of a church that is established upon truth? Jesus said, "You shall know the truth, and the truth shall make you free" (John 8:32).

CHAPTER REVIEW

Answers to the following questions can be found within this chapter.

STUDY QUESTIONS

1. According to 1 Timothy 3:15, "the house of God, which is the church of the living God," is also the "pillar and ground of the

   _____."

2. According to the verse below, the church is the _____ of God, and His Spirit dwells within them.

   Do you not know that you are the temple of God and that the Spirit of God dwells in you? (1 Corinthians 3:16).

3. According to the verses below, the house of God also has a unique membership composed of people who simply wear the

   name _____ and seek to glorify Him with this name.

   And when he had found him, he brought him to Antioch. So it was that for a whole year they assembled with the church and taught a great many people. And the disciples were first called Christians in Antioch (Acts 11:26).

But if a man suffer as a Christian, let him not be ashamed; but let him glorify God in this name (1 Peter 4:16, American Standard Version*).*

FOCUS QUESTIONS

1. According to Colossians 1:17-18, Who is the head of the church? _____

2. The Lord's house can be distinguished from other would-be houses by its unique _____.

3. If one follows the blueprint found in the New Testament, could the house of God (the church of Christ) be established today? YES / NO

An ANSWER KEY for the STUDY QUESTIONS and FOCUS QUESTIONS is provided in the back of the book.

THINGS YOU SHOULD KNOW

- The church is the house of God.
- Jesus is the builder of the church.
- Jesus has all authority over His church.
- The church built by Christ wears the name of Christ.
- The church built by Christ is organized with elders (also known as bishops, pastors, overseers, presbyters, and shepherds).
- The church built by Jesus worships without the accompaniment of mechanical instruments of music.
- The church built by Jesus partakes of the Lord's Supper every first day of the week.
- The only "creed book" used by the house of God is the Bible.
- The church built by Jesus has a unique doctrine, work, membership, and priesthood.

DIGGING DEEPER

The material below is intended for those people who would like to study this subject further. It contains information that was not necessarily discussed in the lesson.

CONCERNING THE CHURCH (OR KINGDOM)

...The time is fulfilled, and the kingdom of God is at hand. Repent, and believe in the gospel (Mark 1:15).

And He said to them, "Assuredly, I say to you that there are some standing here who will not taste death till they see the kingdom of God present with power" (Mark 9:1).

Then Paul dwelt two whole years in his own rented house, and received all who came to him, preaching the kingdom of God and teaching the things which concern the Lord Jesus Christ with all confidence, no one forbidding him (Acts 28:30-31).

To the church of God which is at Corinth, to those who are sanctified in Christ Jesus, called to be saints... (1 Corinthians 1:2).

Then comes the end, when He delivers the kingdom to God the Father, when He puts an end to all rule and all authority and power. For He must reign till He has put all enemies under His feet (1 Corinthians 15:24-25).

He has delivered us from the power of darkness and conveyed us into the kingdom of the Son of His love (Colossians 1:13).

These things I write to you, though I hope to come to you shortly; but if I am delayed, I write so that you may know how you ought to conduct yourself in the house of God, which is the church of the living God, the pillar and ground of the truth (1 Timothy 3:14-15).

THINGS TO THINK ABOUT...WHEN DIGGING DEEPER

1. Did Jesus teach in Mark 1:15 that the church (the kingdom) was "far away" from the people to whom He spoke? YES / NO

2. In Mark 9:1, did Jesus say that some of the people to whom He spoke would be alive when the kingdom of God arrived? YES / NO

3. According to Acts 28:30-31, what did Paul preach to those who

About the House of God

came to visit him while he was under house arrest in Rome?

_____   _____   _____

_____

4. At the end of time, the Lord will deliver something to His Father (1 Corinthians 15:24-25). What is that something?

_____   _____

5. Did Paul tell Timothy (1 Timothy 3:14-15) that "the house of God" and "the church" are the same? YES / NO

CONCERNING THE MEMBERS OF THE CHURCH

Blessed are you when they revile and persecute you, and say all kinds of evil against you falsely for My sake. Rejoice and be exceedingly glad, for great is your reward in heaven, for so they persecuted the prophets who were before you (Matthew 5:11-12).

And you will be hated by all for My name's sake. But he who endures to the end will be saved (Matthew 10:22).

The world cannot hate you, but it hates Me because I testify of it that its works are evil (John 7:7).

If the world hates you, you know that it hated Me before it hated you (John 15:18).

...And the disciples were first called Christians in Antioch (Acts 11:26).

This I also did in Jerusalem, and many of the saints I shut up in prison, having received authority from the chief priests; and when they were put to death, I cast my vote against them. And I punished them often in every synagogue and compelled them to blaspheme; and being exceedingly enraged against them, I persecuted them even to foreign cities (Acts 26:10-11).

Then Agrippa said to Paul, "You almost persuade me to become a Christian" (Acts 26:28).

For you have heard of my former conduct in Judaism, how I persecuted the church of God beyond measure and tried to destroy it (Galatians 1:13).

Yet if anyone suffers as a Christian, let him not be ashamed, but let him glorify God in this matter (1 Peter 4:16).

6. In such passages as Matthew 5:11-12, John 15:18, and Matthew 10:22, did Christ say that His followers would be viewed and treated favorably by most people in the world? YES / NO

7. What were Christ's disciples called "first" in the city of Antioch? _____

8. According to Acts 26:28, was the name "Christian" ever used by pagan rulers to refer to Christ's disciples? YES / NO

9. Did Peter, as an apostle of the Lord, use the name "Christian" (1 Peter 4:16) to refer to Christ's disciples? YES / NO

10. In Galatians 1:13, Paul said that he persecuted "the church of God." In Acts 26:10-11, however, he said that he persecuted "the saints." Of what, then, must the church be composed?

_____

11. According to Acts 11:26, what would be another name for those "saints"? _____

CONCERNING THE LEADERS OF AND OFFICES IN THE CHURCH

Therefore take heed to yourselves and to all the flock, among which the Holy Spirit has made you overseers, to shepherd the church of God which He purchased with His own blood (Acts 20:28).

Likewise deacons must be reverent, not double-tongued, not given to much wine, not greedy for money, holding the mystery of the faith with a pure conscience. But let these also first be tested; then let them serve as deacons, being found blameless. Likewise, their wives must be reverent, not slanderers, temperate, faithful in all things. Let deacons be the husbands of one wife, ruling their children and their own houses well. For those who have served well as deacons obtain for themselves a good standing and great boldness in the faith which is in Christ Jesus (1 Timothy 3:8-13).

Let the elders who rule well be counted worthy of double honor, especially those who labor in the word and doctrine (1 Timothy 5:17).

For this reason I left you in Crete, that you should set in order the things that are lacking, and appoint elders in every city as I commanded you—if a man is blameless, the husband of one wife, having faithful children not accused of dissipation or insubordination. For a bishop must be blameless, as a steward of God, not self-willed, not quick-tempered, not given to wine, not violent, not greedy for money, but hospitable, a lover of what is good, sober-minded, just, holy, self-controlled, holding fast the faithful word as he has been taught, that he may be able, by sound doctrine, both to exhort and convict those who contradict (Titus 1:5-9).

Remember those who rule over you, who have spoken the word of God to you, whose faith follow, considering the outcome of their *conduct (Hebrews 13:7).*

THINGS TO THINK ABOUT...WHEN DIGGING DEEPER

12. According to Titus 1:5-9, is it God's will that the church have elders (pastors, shepherds, overseers, bishops)? YES / NO

13. Does Acts 20:28 teach that the overseers of God's church are to look after the spiritual welfare of the Christians who compose the church? YES / NO

14. According to Titus 1:5-9, must the men who serve as elders (pastors, shepherds, overseers, bishops) meet certain qualifications as set forth by God in His word? YES / NO

15. Did Paul tell Timothy that it was God's will that a church have servants known as "deacons" (1 Timothy 3:8-13)? YES / NO

16. According to 1 Timothy 3:8-13, must the men who serve as deacons (servants) meet certain qualifications as set forth by God in His word? YES / NO

17. According to Hebrews 13:7, should Christians respect and obey those elders (overseers) who "rule over" the church? YES / NO

CONCERNING THE WORSHIP OF THE CHURCH

God is Spirit, and those who worship Him must worship in spirit and truth (John 4:24).

Preaching...

Whatever I tell you in the dark, speak in the light; and what you hear in the ear, preach on the housetops (Matthew 10:27).

And He commanded us to preach to the people, and to testify that it is He who was ordained by God to be Judge of the living and the dead (Acts 10:42).

About the House of God

How then shall they call on Him in whom they have not believed? And how shall they believe in Him of whom they have not heard? And how shall they hear without a preacher? And how shall they preach unless they are sent? As it is written: "How beautiful are the feet of those who preach the gospel of peace, Who bring glad tidings of good things!" (Romans 10:14-15).

For we do not preach ourselves, but Christ Jesus the Lord, and ourselves your bondservants for Jesus' sake (2 Corinthians 4:5).

Preach the word! Be ready in season and *out of season. Convince, rebuke, exhort, with all longsuffering and teaching (2 Timothy 4:2).*

Praying...

So Jesus answered and said to them, "Assuredly, I say to you, if you have faith and do not doubt, you will not only do what was done to the fig tree, but also if you say to this mountain, 'Be removed and be cast into the sea,' it will be done. And whatever things you ask in prayer, believing, you will receive" (Matthew 21:21-22).

Now in the morning, having risen a long while before daylight, He went out and departed to a solitary place; and there He prayed (Mark 1:35).

I do not pray for these alone, but also for those who will believe in Me through their word; that they all may be one, as You, Father, are in Me, and I in You; that they also may be one in Us, that the world may believe that You sent Me (John 17:20-21).

Continue earnestly in prayer, being vigilant in it with thanksgiving (Colossians 4:2).

Confess your *trespasses to one another, and pray for one another, that you may be healed. The effective, fervent prayer of a righteous man avails much (James 5:16).*

Giving...

Now concerning the collection for the saints, as I have given orders to the churches of Galatia, so you must do also: On the first day *of the week let each one of you lay something aside, storing up as he may prosper, that there be no collections when I come (1 Corinthians 16:1-2).*

But this I say: *He who sows sparingly will also reap sparingly, and he who sows bountifully will also reap bountifully.* So let *each one* give *as he purposes in his heart, not grudgingly or of necessity; for God loves a cheerful giver (2 Corinthians 9:6-7).*

The Lord's Supper...

When the hour had come, He sat down, and the twelve apostles with Him. Then He said to them, "With fervent *desire I have desired to eat this Passover with you before I suffer; for I say to you, I will no longer eat of it until it is fulfilled in the kingdom of God." Then He took the cup, and gave thanks, and said, "Take this and divide* it *among yourselves; for I say to you, I will not drink of the fruit of the vine until the kingdom of God comes." And He took bread, gave thanks and broke* it, *and gave* it *to them, saying, "This is My body which is given for you; do this in remembrance of Me." Likewise He also* took *the cup after supper, saying, "This cup* is *the new covenant in My blood, which is shed for you" (Luke 22:14-20).*

For I received from the Lord that which I also delivered to you: that the Lord Jesus on the same *night in which He was betrayed took bread; and when He had given thanks, He broke* it *and said, "Take, eat; this is My body which is broken for you; do this in remembrance of Me." In the same manner* He *also* took *the cup after supper, saying, "This cup is the new covenant in My blood. This do, as often as you drink* it, *in remembrance of Me." For as often as you eat this bread and drink this cup, you proclaim the Lord's death till He comes (1 Corinthians 11:23-26).*

Singing...

What is the conclusion *then? I will pray with the spirit, and I will also pray with the understanding. I will sing with the spirit, and I will also sing with the understanding (1 Corinthians 14:15).*

...Be filled with the Spirit, speaking to one another in psalms and hymns and spiritual songs, singing and making melody in your heart to the Lord (Ephesians 5:18-19).

THINGS TO THINK ABOUT...WHEN DIGGING DEEPER

18. According to John 4:24, people must worship God in

    _____ and _____.

19. According to Romans 10:14-15, is preaching important in spreading the Gospel? YES / NO

20. Does 2 Corinthians 4:5 teach that those who preach should not preach about themselves, but about Christ? YES / NO

21. According to 2 Timothy 4:2, Paul told Timothy to be ready

    to preach _____ season and _____

    _____ season.

22. According to Mark 1:35 and John 17:20-21, was prayer important to Jesus Christ? YES / NO

23. According to Colossians 4:2, Christians should _____

    _____ in prayer.

24. Does James 5:16 teach that the prayer of a righteous Christian is effective? YES / NO

25. According to 1 Corinthians 16:1-2, a Christian is to give back to the Lord "as he may _____."

26. In 2 Corinthians 9:6-7, Paul taught that God loves a

    _____ _____.

27. According to Luke 22:14-20, was the Lord's Supper established by man? YES / NO

28. According to 1 Corinthians 11:23-26, when Christians partake of the Lord's Supper, what are they proclaiming?

    _____ _____ _____.

29. According to 1 Corinthians 14:15, Christians are to sing with

    the _____.

30. In Ephesians 5:18-19, the "instrument" that Paul commands each Christian to make "melody in" is his _____.

CONCERNING THE WORKS OF THE CHURCH

Evangelism...

Then He said to His disciples, "The harvest truly is plentiful, but the laborers are few. Therefore pray the Lord of the harvest to send out laborers into His harvest" (Matthew 9:37-38).

Go therefore and make disciples of all the nations, baptizing them in the name of the Father and of the Son and of the Holy Spirit, teaching them to observe all things that I have commanded you; and lo, I am with you always, even to the end of the age (Matthew 28:19-20).

And He said to them, "Go into all the world and preach the gospel to every creature" (Mark 16:15).

Therefore do not be ashamed of the testimony of our Lord...who has saved us and called us with a holy calling, not according to our works, but according to His own purpose and grace which was given to us in Christ Jesus before time began, but has now been revealed by the appearing of our Savior Jesus Christ, who has abolished death and brought life and immortality to light through the gospel (2 Timothy 1:8-10).

Edification...

For he who serves Christ in these things is acceptable to God and approved by men. Therefore let us pursue the things which make for peace and the things by which one may edify another (Romans 14:18-19).

Therefore comfort each other and edify one another, just as you also are doing. And we urge you, brethren, to recognize those who labor among you, and are over you in the Lord and admonish you, and to esteem them very highly in love for their work's sake. Be at peace among yourselves (1 Thessalonians 5:11-13).

Benevolence...

Therefore, whatever you want men to do to you, do also to them... (Matthew 7:12).

"And you shall love the LORD Your God with all your heart, with all your soul, with all your mind, and with all your strength." This is the first commandment. And the second, like it, is this: "You shall love your neighbor as yourself." There is no other commandment greater than these (Mark 12:30-31).

Therefore, as we have opportunity, let us do good to all, especially to those who are of the household of faith (Galatians 6:10).

About the House of God

THINGS TO THINK ABOUT…WHEN DIGGING DEEPER

31. Each of Jesus' disciples should be concerned about carrying out evangelism because "the harvest is truly _____, but the laborers are _____" (Matthew 9:37-38).

32. In Matthew 28:19-20 and Mark 16:15, did Jesus command His followers to teach the Gospel to the rest of the world? YES / NO

33. In 2 Timothy 1:8-10, Paul spoke of the fact that through the Gospel, Jesus abolished _____ and brought _____.

34. "Therefore let us pursue the things which make for _____ and the things by which one may _____ another" (Romans 14:19).

35. According to 1 Thessalonians 5:11-13, are Christians told to recognize and esteem their elders (bishops, overseers)? YES / NO

36. Does Matthew 7:12 teach that we have to actively do to others what we want them to do to us? YES / NO

37. In the last part of Mark 12:30-31, Christians are told to love God and to love their neighbors because "there is no other commandment _____ than these."

38. Does Galatians 6:10 teach that Christians can only help people who are Christians? YES / NO

CONCERNING THE DOCTRINE OF THE CHURCH

Jesus answered them and said, "My doctrine is not Mine, but His who sent Me. If anyone wills to do His will, he shall know concerning the doctrine, whether it is from God or whether I speak on My own authority" (John 7:16-17).

But God be thanked that though you were slaves of sin, yet you obeyed from the heart that form of doctrine to which you were delivered. And having been set free from sin, you became slaves of righteousness (Romans 6:17-18).

That we should no longer be children, tossed to and fro and carried about with every wind of doctrine, by the trickery of men, in the cunning craftiness of deceitful plotting, but, speaking the truth in love, may grow up in all things into Him who is the head—Christ—from whom the whole body, joined and knit together by what every joint supplies, according to the effective working by which every part does its share, causes growth of the body for the edifying of itself in love (Ephesians 4:14-16).

If you instruct the brethren in these things, you will be a good minister of Jesus Christ, nourished in the words of faith and of the good doctrine which you have carefully followed (1 Timothy 4:6).

Till I come, give attention to reading, to exhortation, to doctrine (1 Timothy 4:13).

Take heed to yourself and to the doctrine. Continue in them, for in doing this you will save both yourself and those who hear you (1 Timothy 4:16).

If anyone teaches otherwise and does not consent to wholesome words, even *the words of our Lord Jesus Christ, and to the doctrine which accords with godliness, he is proud, knowing nothing, but is obsessed with disputes and arguments over words, from which come envy, strife, reviling, evil suspicions (1 Timothy 6:3-4).*

For the time will come when they will not endure sound doctrine, but according to their own desires, because they have itching ears, they will heap up for themselves teachers; and they will turn their ears away from the truth, and be turned aside to fables (2 Timothy 4:3-4).

But as for you, speak the things which are proper for sound doctrine (Titus 2:1).

Likewise, exhort the young men to be sober-minded, in all things showing yourself to be a pattern of good works; in doctrine showing integrity, reverence, incorruptibility, sound speech that cannot be condemned, that one who is an opponent may be ashamed, having nothing evil to say of you (Titus 2:6-8).

Whoever transgresses and does not abide in the doctrine of Christ does not have God. He who abides in the doctrine of Christ has both the Father and the Son. If anyone comes to you and does not bring this doctrine, do not receive him into your house nor greet him; for he who greets him shares in his evil deeds (2 John 9-11).

THINGS TO THINK ABOUT...WHEN DIGGING DEEPER

39. According to John 7:16-17, the doctrine that Jesus taught originated with _____.

40. According to Romans 6:17-18, is obedience to the doctrine of Christ important? YES / NO

41. In Ephesians 4:14-16, one good reason for knowing and abiding by the doctrine that Jesus taught is that it will help prevent us from being tossed _____ _____ _____.

42. 1 Timothy 4:6 says that we should be "nourished in the _____ of faith."

43. In 1 Timothy 4:13, Timothy was told to pay strict attention to reading, exhortation, and _____.

44. In 1 Timothy 4:16, Timothy was told that taking heed to the doctrine was important because this is how he could _____ himself and those that heard him.

45. According to 1 Timothy 6:3-4, a person who does not teach Christ's doctrine in a faithful manner is _____ and knows _____.

46. "Speak the things which are proper for _____ _____" (Titus 2:1).

47. According to Titus 2:6-8, four things we are to exhibit in regard to doctrine are _____, _____, _____, and _____ _____.

48. According to 2 John 9-11, if we do not abide in the doctrine of Christ, can we have a relationship with God the Father and Jesus? YES / NO

CONCERNING THE CHRISTIAN'S MEDIATOR AND ADVOCATE

For there is one God and one Mediator between God and men, the Man Christ Jesus, who gave Himself a ransom for all, to be testified in due time (1 Timothy 2:5-6).

But now He has obtained a more excellent ministry, inasmuch as He is also Mediator of a better covenant, which was established on better promises (Hebrews 8:6).

And for this reason He is the Mediator of the new covenant, by means of death, for the redemption of the transgressions under the first covenant, that those who are called may receive the promise of the eternal inheritance (Hebrews 9:15).

My little children, these things I write to you, so that you may not sin. And if anyone sins, we have an Advocate with the Father, Jesus Christ the righteous. And He Himself is the propitiation [substitutionary sacrifice] for our sins, and not for ours only but also for the whole world (1 John 2:1-2).

THINGS TO THINK ABOUT...WHEN DIGGING DEEPER

49. According to 1 Timothy 2:5-6, how many mediators are there between God and man? _____

50. According to 1 Timothy 2:5-6, Who is the Mediator between God and man? _____ _____

51. According to Hebrews 9:15, did Jesus have to die before he could become our Mediator? YES / NO

52. Hebrews 9:15 says that as Mediator, Christ makes it possible for us to receive the promise of the _____ _____.

53. According to 1 John 2:1-2, Christians have an Advocate Who pleads their case before God. Who is that Advocate? _____ _____

54. 1 John 2:1-2 teaches that Jesus gave himself as a sacrifice for the _____ of the whole world.

An ANSWER KEY for the DIGGING DEEPER QUESTIONS is provided in the back of the book.

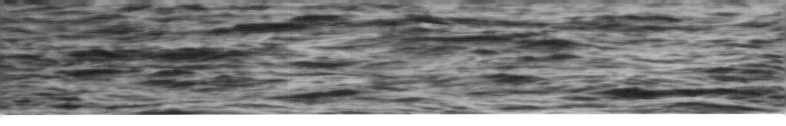

Searching for Truth

ABOUT BAPTISM

In today's world, there are many differing viewpoints about baptism. Some say that babies should be baptized, while others say that it is reserved only for adults. Some believe that baptism is necessary for salvation, while others do not. What is the truth about baptism? Have you ever wondered about whether or not you needed to be baptized? And, if you have been baptized, was your baptism for the right reason as described in the Bible?

INTRODUCTION

Water! It is one of our most precious resources. Without it, the world as we know it would not exist. We have to have it to sustain life. It quenches our thirst, it can make us clean, and it can make us feel like a new person after a hard day's work. Is it any wonder then, that in the Bible, water is used by God as an important element and symbol for purification and cleansing?

Whether it was the flood of Noah that cleansed the Earth, the ritual purification for cleansing in Judaism, or the baptism of thousands in the New Testament, water was a very important part of God's plan in saving souls.

But how, and why, was it a part of God's plan? Why *were* believers baptized in water? And is it necessary that a person be baptized *today* for salvation? If so, what does a person need to know *before* he or she can be baptized?

Before we begin our search, it would be helpful if you would answer several very important questions. Write your response below each of the following questions.

- **Are you now in a saved relationship with God? In other words, if you were to die today, would you go to heaven or hell?**
    ☐ YES
    ☐ NO
    ☐ I DO NOT KNOW

- **If you are *not now* in a saved relationship with God, were you at some point in the past?**
    ☐ NO
    ☐ IN THE PAST, BUT NOT NOW
    ☐ I DO NOT KNOW

- **If you are now saved, or if you were saved at some point in the past, *how* did you become saved?** In other words, what did you do or say to become a Christian?

_____

_____

_____

- **Have you ever been baptized? If you have, was it done by sprinkling, pouring, or immersion?**
    ☐ YES, I HAVE BEEN BAPTIZED BY
        ☐ SPRINKLING
        ☐ POURING
        ☐ IMMERSION
    ☐ NO, I HAVE NOT BEEN BAPTIZED

- **If you were baptized, were you baptized as a child or as one who was mature?** In other words, were you baptized as a baby or as an adult?
    ☐ I WAS BAPTIZED AS A CHILD
    ☐ I WAS BAPTIZED AS ONE WHO WAS MATURE

- **Were you saved *before* your baptism or *after* your baptism?**
    ☐ I WAS SAVED BEFORE BAPTISM
    ☐ I WAS SAVED AFTER BAPTISM

- **What was the *purpose* of your baptism?**

_____

_____

_____

_____

With those questions answered, let us begin our search for the truth about baptism. As we study the Bible, let me encourage you to

About Baptism

think seriously about your relationship with God, because if you are not yet saved, in this session we will be examining what you need to do to *become* saved. However, if you feel you are already saved, let me encourage you to compare the answers you gave to the six questions above to the information in this lesson—to see if what you have been *taught* is consistent and in keeping with *the word of God.*

Remember, as we have observed over and over again, *truth* is what will make you free (John 8:32). The commandments of men and the traditions of men will not make you free; neither will good intentions nor a sincere attitude, in and of themselves, make you free. Only Jesus and the power of His word can set you free. So let us go in search of the truth to see what we can discover about baptism, and in so doing, let us answer these four important questions:

1. **What is baptism?**
2. **What is the purpose of baptism?**
3. **Who should be baptized?**
4. **Have *you* been *scripturally* baptized?**

Let us begin with the first question: "What *is* baptism?"

WHAT IS BAPTISM?

Baptism is immersion. It is a word that was used rather commonly in New Testament times, and not always just in a religious sense. When a ship sank, for example, it was "baptized." The Scriptures do speak of more than one type of baptism, such as the baptism of John, the baptism of fire, and the baptism of the Holy Spirit. Primarily, however, we need to center our thoughts on the type of baptism that applies to all of us. When we look into the Scriptures, they will tell us something of the nature of that baptism. It is obviously something done in water. Biblical references to people "going down into" and "coming up out of" the water document that quite well.

Kenneth Ratcliff
Elder

Consider, for example, what happened in the first century when an evangelist by the name of Philip taught a man of Ethiopia how to become a Christian. That story is recorded in Acts 8. There, we learn that the Ethiopian was on his way from Jerusalem, going toward Gaza. He was sitting in his chariot, and was reading from the Old Testament book of Isaiah. It was at this point that Philip entered and heard him reading from Isaiah 53 about a servant of

God Who would suffer on behalf of sinners. While reading about the sacrificial nature of this suffering, the Ethiopian said to Philip: "I ask you, of whom does the prophet say this, of himself or of some other man?" (Acts 8:34). Notice how Philip responded:

Then Philip opened his mouth, and beginning at this Scripture, preached Jesus to him (Acts 8:35).

From this passage, we can see that Philip taught the Ethiopian about Jesus. Teaching someone about Jesus includes teaching them about the Lord's deity, His power, His love, and His death, burial and resurrection. Notice the immediate response to the preaching about Jesus:

Now as they went down the road, they came to some water. And the eunuch said, "See, here is water. What hinders me from being baptized?" Then Philip said, "If you believe with all your heart, you may." And he answered and said, "I believe that Jesus Christ is the Son of God." So he commanded the chariot to stand still. And both Philip and the eunuch went down into the water, and he baptized him (Acts 8:36-38).

In this account, we learn not only that baptism was a part of preaching about Jesus, but we also learn something about the mode or manner of baptism. In this instance, it required both Philip and the Ethiopian to *go down into* the water. It was then, after they were in the water, that Philip baptized the Ethiopian.

Thus, when one is immersed, he or she is plunged beneath the water and is completely covered. In fact, the person is *buried*—which is exactly how the apostle Paul describes baptism:

Or do you not know that as many of us as were baptized into Christ Jesus were baptized into His death? Therefore we were buried with Him through baptism into death, that just as Christ was raised from the dead by the glory of the Father, even so we also should walk in newness of life (Romans 6:3-4).

In reference to this passage, Adam Clarke, a well-known Bible scholar and preacher from the Methodist Church, concluded as well that New Testament baptism was done by immersion:

Alluding to the immersion practiced in the case of adults, wherein the person appeared to be buried under the water as Christ was buried in the heart of the Earth, His rising again the third day, and their emerging from the water, was an emblem of the resurrection of the body (*Adam Clarke's Commentary* on Colossians 2:12).

Notice also how John Calvin, the founder of the Presbyterian Church, described baptism:

The very word "baptize," however, signifies to immerse, and it is certain that immersion was the practice of the ancient church (*Institutes of the Christian Religion*, Book IV, Chap. 15, Sect. 19, trans. by John Allen, Philadelphia:Nicklin and Howe, 1816).

Today, there are many churches that have adopted the practices of sprinkling or pouring as forms of baptism. Yet, nowhere in the New Testament is this practice of sprinkling or pouring connected with baptism.

Sprinkling or pouring water on someone as a form of baptism is not a part of authentic Christianity. In the Greek language, which was the language in which the New Testament was originally written, there were words for both sprinkling and pouring. The word for sprinkling is *rhaino*, and would be used for the sprinkling of blood, for example. The word for pouring is *cheo*. Although both of these words were available to the writers of the New Testament, they are never used in connection with baptism. Instead the word used in association with baptism is *baptisma*, which has the root meaning of submerge, plunge, or immerse.

Rick Brumback
Bible Instructor and Minister

You might ask, as some have, whether or not there was a sufficient amount of water available in the land of Palestine in the first century to immerse the large numbers of people who (as recorded in Acts 2 and in John 3) were being baptized.

First of all, let me say that baptism does not require a great amount of water. Baptism by immersion has been done in some very small places, such as bathtubs or watering troughs.

Second, I would add that in the first century, sufficient water was available, both in the rivers and streams of Palestine, as well as in the many water-collection systems built by the people of the ancient world.

Third, because of the Jewish emphasis upon ritual cleansing, many hundreds of baptistries (known as *miqvehs*) were already in place in and around major cities and places of worship. In Jerusalem alone, archaeologists have discovered approximately 150 of them dating to the time Christ.

So in answering our first major question, "What is baptism?," we must conclude that the baptism required of sinners in the New Testament was done by immersion (plunging someone into water). It was not done by sprinkling or pouring.

About Baptism

SECTION REVIEW: *WHAT IS BAPTISM?*

Answers to the following questions can be found in the section above.

STUDY QUESTIONS

1. Water is used by God as an important element and symbol for _____ and cleansing.

2. According to Acts 8:38, when Philip baptized the Ethiopian eunuch, both he and the eunuch "went _____ _____ the water."

3. According to Romans 6:3-4, is baptism described as a burial? YES / NO

4. It is certain that immersion (i.e. baptism) was the practice of the early church. YES / NO

5. The Greek word for "sprinkling" is *rhaino.* Is it ever used in the New Testament in association with baptism? YES / NO

6. The Greek word for "pouring" is *cheo.* Is it ever used in the New Testament in association with baptism? YES / NO

7. The Greek word *baptisma* has the root meaning of submerge, plunge, or _____.

8. Because of Jewish emphasis upon ritual cleansing, there were hundreds of _____ (known as *miqvehs*) in place in and around major cities and places of worship during the first century.

An ANSWER KEY for the STUDY QUESTIONS is provided in the back of the book.

DECISION POINTS

A. If you have been baptized, were you baptized *correctly,* according to the New Testament pattern? YES / NO

B. If a person was "baptized" by sprinkling or pouring, was he or she baptized correctly, according to the New Testament? YES / NO

TALKING POINTS

A. Discuss the significance of the fact that baptism is a full-body immersion, in light of Paul's comments in Romans 6:3-4.

B. If a person has been "baptized" by sprinkling or pouring, and if he or she comes to realize that the baptism was not scriptural, what should be done about it?

C. What did John Calvin and Adam Clarke believe about the mode of baptism? Why has this view about the mode of baptism changed among various denominations?

WHAT IS THE PURPOSE OF BAPTISM?

Now, let us answer the question, "What is the *purpose* of baptism?" *Why* were sinners being baptized? Was there something magical or mystical about the water that regenerated sinners? Again, let us go to the Bible as our guide for ascertaining the truth, and as we search its pages, let us notice how God used both the elements of blood and water as a means for spiritual cleansing and purification throughout three distinct periods of time and systems of religion.

Those periods of time and systems of religion are known as the Patriarchal Age (approximately 4000 B.C.), the Mosaic Age (approximately 1500 B.C.), and the Christian Age (approximately A.D. 33). In the Patriarchal period, water was used to cleanse the Earth and to save Noah and his family from destruction. Those floodwaters were spoken of by Peter as a figure for baptism in the Christian Age.

> *Who formerly were disobedient, when once the Divine longsuffering waited in the days of Noah, while* the *ark was being prepared, in which a few, that is, eight souls, were saved through water. There is also an antitype which now saves us—baptism (not the removal of the filth of the flesh, but the answer of a good conscience toward God), through the resurrection of Jesus Christ (1 Peter 3:20-21).*

Also in the Patriarchal Age, the blood of animals was used as a symbol for justification and covenant, as in the cases of Abel, Noah, and Abraham.

During the Mosaic Age, God used blood as a symbol for purifi-cation and redemption—as in the story of the Exodus when God saved the nation of Israel from the death of their firstborn by passing over the doors of those who had placed blood on their doorposts (Exodus 12). Especially in the book of Leviticus is the use of blood emphasized, as blood was sprinkled on the altar, on the priest, and occasionally on the people.

In addition, water was used as a symbol of purification and cleansing during the Mosaic Age. It was used for the purpose of purifying the priest who came to serve in the temple or tabernacle (Leviticus 8:6). It also was used to purify the cleansed leper who was seeking readmittance into the camp of Israel. The use of these two elements under each of these two systems served as a basis and foundation for their use in the New Testament era.

Under the Christian Age, Jesus shed *His* precious blood for the purpose of purification and cleansing. He was scourged. He was ridiculed. Then He was crucified on the cruel cross of Calvary. It was on that cross that He shed His blood. His blood was pure and innocent, and was offered as a payment to purchase our freedom from the slavery of sin.

> *Knowing that you were not redeemed with corruptible things,* like *silver or gold, from your aimless conduct re-*ceived *by tradition from your fathers, but with the precious blood of Christ, as of a lamb without blemish and without spot (1 Peter 1:18-19).*

Not only does the blood of Jesus redeem, but it also justifies:

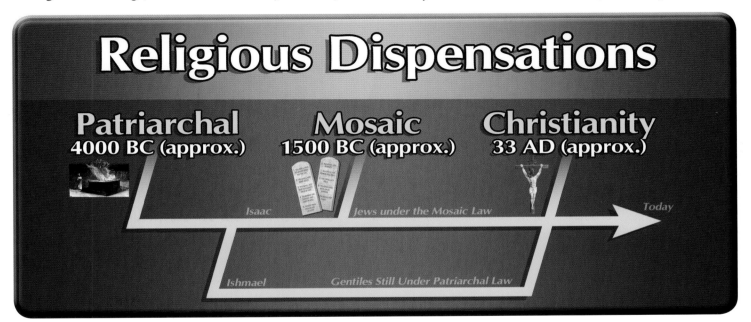

About Baptism

For all have sinned and fall short of the glory of God, being justified freely by His grace through the redemption that is in Christ Jesus, whom God set forth as a propitiation by His blood, through faith, to demonstrate His righteousness, because in His forbearance God had passed over the sins that were previously committed, to demonstrate at the present time His righteousness, that He might be just and the justifier of the one who has faith in Jesus (Romans 3:23-26).

The word "justification" is indeed an intriguing word, and shows conclusively how much God loves all men everywhere. The word "justified" in the original text carries with it the idea of being "not guilty" or "acquitted." Thus, there is a point in time—when we come in contact with the blood of Christ—when God can say that man is no longer guilty of sin. He has been "justified."

Norman Starling
Evangelist

Most assuredly, the blood of Jesus saves. Yet, just as God in the Old Testament used *both* blood *and* water in purifying and cleansing, He likewise uses today, under the New Covenant, *both* blood *and* water to justify the sinner.

To better understand this relationship between blood and water, let us turn our attention to the book of Romans, where the Holy Spirit revealed how the blood of Jesus and the waters of baptism work together to bring about salvation. In Romans 1, the apostle Paul reminds his readers that the Gospel—the message contained within the Bible—is God's power unto salvation. In chapters 2 and 3, he reminds them that "all have sinned and fall short of the glory of God" (Romans 3:23).

The word "all" in this passage refers to all classes and nationalities of people. We go on to learn in this same chapter, as well as in chapter 5, that all of these people can be justified and saved from God's wrath by the blood of Christ. But when we come to chapter 6, we learn *how* sinners are saved, and how a Christian should live after being saved.

But God be thanked that though you were slaves of sin, yet you obeyed from the heart that form of doctrine to which you were delivered. And having been set free from sin, you became slaves of righteousness (Romans 6:17-18).

Here we see that those who were servants of sin had become servants of righteousness. What made the difference? What made them free from sin? How did they gain access to the cleansing blood of Christ? In other words, *what did they do to become Christians?*

First of all, let us notice that *they were obedient.* They did not just "believe" on the name of Jesus to be freed from their past sins, because *faith alone cannot save.* True *saving* faith involves *works.*

It involves *doing* the will of God.

You believe that there is one God. You do well. Even the demons believe—and tremble! But do you want to know, O foolish man, that faith without works is dead? ... You see then that a man is justified by works, and not by faith only (James 2:19-20,24).

Notice what James said. He stated that a man is justified *by works,* and *not by faith alone.* Jesus also confirmed the necessity of obedience.

Not everyone who says to Me, "Lord, Lord," shall enter the kingdom of heaven, but he who does the will of My Father in heaven (Matthew 7:21).

Merely crying out to the Lord, or even boasting of what we have done in the name of Christ, is not sufficient. Jesus said we must *do* the will of the Father. While the works and commandments of men cannot save, the works of God can!

For everyone practicing evil hates the light and does not come to the light, lest his deeds should be exposed. But he who does the truth comes to the light, that his deeds may be clearly seen, that they have been done in God (John 3:20-21).

When we do what the truth says, we come to the light. Obeying the truth reveals that God is saving the sinner. None of us can—by ourselves, or in and of ourselves—save ourselves. But when truth is obeyed, it results in God saving the sinner. Again, in Romans 6 we find that these sinners at Rome were made free from sin *after* they were obedient.

Now, let us notice *what* they obeyed. What did they *do* to be free from sin? Listen again to the apostle Paul:

But God be thanked that though you were slaves of sin, yet you obeyed from the heart that form of doctrine to which you were delivered (Romans 6:17).

What did they obey? They obeyed the *form of doctrine* that had been delivered to them. But what was that doctrine? What had they been taught? Paul tells us:

Moreover, brethren, I declare to you the gospel which I preached to you, which also you received and in which you stand, by which also you are saved, if you hold fast that word which I preached to you—unless you believed in vain. For I delivered to you first of all that which I also received: that Christ died for our sins according to the Scriptures, and that He was buried, and that He rose again the third day according to the Scriptures (1 Corinthians 15:1-4).

As in Romans 6, here in 1 Corinthians 15 Paul makes reference to something that had been delivered (or entrusted) to Christians. What was it? It was his preaching about the death, burial, and resurrection of Christ. These three facts are fundamental to understanding the Gospel of Jesus. They are fundamental to securing salvation for the sinner.

The message of the death, burial, and resurrection was central to what Paul and the others preached in the first century. Concerning Christ's death, they spoke of His scourging and horrible crucifixion. They also emphasized the blood that He shed.

> *But God demonstrates His own love toward us, in that while we were still sinners, Christ died for us. Much more then, having now been justified by His blood, we shall be saved from wrath through Him (Romans 5:8-9).*

> **The law says we must die for our sins. But Jesus says, "I will take the place of sinful man." He, for a time, was separated from God. He satisfied the justice of God for man so that all people who, by faith, reach the blood of Jesus can be justified—declared "not guilty" and "free from sin."**

> Norman Starling
> Evangelist

Not only did the Gospel message include the news about the death and blood of Jesus, but it also included a detailed account of His burial. It told of how Joseph of Arimathea and Nicodemus took the body of Jesus from the cross and prepared it for burial. It told of how they placed the Lord's body in a tomb, and how our Lord's body lay in that burial chamber until Sunday morning when He was resurrected by the power of God. His resurrection meant that He had conquered death, and that He was indeed the Messiah. The Gospel message reveals how Christ victoriously conquered Satan, sin, and the grave. By means of this victory, Jesus bridged the gap between God and the sinner.

According to Isaiah 59:1-2, sin is what separates a person from God. But by means of Christ's death, burial, and resurrection, sinners now have the hope of walking across that bridge and being reunited with God. However, when sinners are obedient to the form of doctrine revealed in the Bible—that is, the death, the burial, and the resurrection of Christ—does that mean that the sinner himself has to *literally* die, *literally* be buried, and *literally* be resurrected in order to be obedient? Read Romans 6:17 once more to learn exactly what it is that sinners must obey:

> *But God be thanked that though you were slaves of sin, yet you obeyed from the heart that form of doctrine to which you were delivered (Romans 6:17).*

What they had obeyed was not the doctrine (or teaching) about the death, burial, and resurrection of Jesus, but a *form* (or pattern) of that doctrine. They obeyed something *like* that doctrine. What was it, and did it involve water? Read what Paul said on this matter:

> *Or do you not know that as many of us as were baptized into Christ Jesus were baptized into His death? Therefore we were buried with Him through baptism into death, that just as Christ was raised from the dead by the glory of the Father, even so we also should walk in newness of life. For if we have been united together in the likeness of His death, certainly we also shall be in the likeness of His resurrection (Romans 6:3-5).*

It is here, in this passage, that we learn how justification and forgiveness are acquired, and how the death of Christ and His blood are intertwined with the waters of baptism. In Romans 6, we learn how sinners at Rome became Christians, for just as Jesus had died on the cross, these Christians chose to die to the old man of sin by confessing Jesus as Lord. Just as Jesus was buried in a grave or tomb, so these sinners were buried in a watery grave of baptism. And, just as Jesus was resurrected by the power of God to a new life, these sinners were brought forth out of baptism by

The Gospel Enacted

1 Corinthians 15:3-4

Jesus the Christ
His Death, Burial and Resurrection
For the Sins of Man

Death

Burial

Resurrection

The Gospel Re-enacted

in Baptism
(Obeying The Gospel)
Romans 6:3-4

In Baptism
We Repent of Sin and Die to Sin
We are Buried in Water for the Remission of Sins
We are Raised to Walk in a New Life

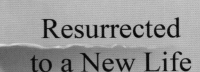

Resurrected
to a New Life

Dead to Sin

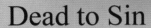

Buried in Water

the same power to walk in newness of life. *Prior* to their baptism, they were spiritually *dead,* but *after* baptism, they were *alive* in Christ; they were in a resurrected state. Baptism, therefore, is for those who are dead in sin. To be spiritually resurrected and made alive in Christ, a sinner must be united with Christ in baptism. The blood of Jesus and the waters of baptism are brought together in a beautiful and life-saving way. Because of this, it should not be a surprise to hear what Jesus said to a believing Jew named Nicodemus.

> *Jesus answered and said to him, "Most assuredly, I say to you, unless one is born again, he cannot see the kingdom of God. ... I say to you, unless one is born of water and the Spirit, he cannot enter the kingdom of God"* (John 3:3,5).

Being born again, and thereby becoming a child of God, *requires* that one be born of the water; that is to say, he or she must be baptized. According to Romans 6:17-18, to be free from sin—and thereby become a servant of righteousness—one must be obedient *in baptism* to the form of doctrine that imitates the death, burial, and resurrection of Christ. In Romans 1:16, we learn that the Gospel is God's power to save. In Romans 6:17, we learn that a form of that Gospel can be obeyed. Since that is true, you and I must come to understand the gravity of the following statement:

> *And to give you who are troubled rest with us when the Lord Jesus is revealed from heaven with His mighty angels, in flaming fire taking vengeance on those who do not know God, and on those who do not obey the gospel of our Lord Jesus Christ* (2 Thessalonians 1:7-8).

The Gospel *must be obeyed!* A sinner cannot save himself or herself by *literally* being crucified, and by *literally* being buried, and by *literally* being resurrected from the grave. But, as we have seen, a sinner *can* do something similar to this. A sinner can be buried with Christ in baptism for the remission of sins (Acts 2:38), and then arise to walk in a new life (Colossians 2:12).

At this point you might be asking, "Can the water itself save?" Is there something magical or mystical about water—particularly water in a baptistry? No, there is nothing in the Bible to suggest that water *by itself* can save a soul from death. The Bible nowhere suggests that water alone can save, but neither does it teach that *faith alone* can save. It is God's grace that saves a person. But it is also God's word, the truth, which tells us *when* a person is saved, and *at what point* that person is in a right relationship with God.

The only way to know if baptism is essential for salvation is to check the biblical record. The text of 1 Peter 3:21 tells us that baptism *does* something. What does it do? Peter says, "There is

also an antitype which now saves us—baptism (not the removal of the filth of the flesh, but the answer of a good conscience toward God), through the resurrection of Jesus Christ." Baptism is not a bath that cleanses us of dirt, but it does give us a good conscience. Plus, it is for the remission of sins (Acts 2:38) and washes away sins (Acts 22:16). The blood of Christ is what washes our sins away (Revelation 1:5). But *when* do we come in contact with that blood? It is when, as penitent, confessing believers, we are baptized.

B. J. Clarke
Minister

This principle of being cleansed by God when we do as He directs can also be seen in the Old Testament story of the Syrian general, Naaman, who was seeking to be cleansed of his leprosy. According to 2 Kings 5:1-14, Naaman, in an attempt to rid himself of this horrible disease, came to the prophet Elisha, hoping to receive some great pronouncement. Instead, Elisha told Naaman to dip himself seven times in the river Jordan. At first, Naaman resisted the idea that the river Jordan could somehow cleanse him. And, indeed, the waters of the Jordan River by themselves could not cleanse a person of leprosy—either then or now. But when that water was coupled with obedience to the command of God, the Syrian general was immediately made whole. His leprosy then, and *only* then, was cured.

Today, no amount of water by itself can save a soul from the leprosy of sin. But when baptism is coupled with a trusting, obedient faith, then God says you can be saved by the blood of Christ. It really is a matter of trusting in *what* God said to do, *when* God said to do it, *how* God said to do it, and *for the reason* God said to do it.

Thus, in answering our question about the purpose of baptism, we have learned that baptism is for the remission of sins, and also is the means by which one becomes a servant of righteousness, a child of God, and a Christian.

For one to be saved and reap an eternal home in heaven, one must be a member of Christ's body. Paul says in Ephesians 1:3 that all spiritual blessings are "in Christ." One of those spiritual blessings is salvation (2 Timothy 2:10). In order for one to have salvation—which is "in Christ"—one must get into Christ. Paul said in 1 Corinthians 12:13, "For by one Spirit we were all baptized into one body."

Alfred Washington
Minister

Baptism places a sinner into the body of Christ (that is to say, the church of Christ), and is the means by which a sinner is clothed with Christ. It is the point in the process of conversion when a sinner can call himself or herself a Christian. Baptism, then, serves a unique and important purpose of which we must be fully aware.

SECTION REVIEW: *WHAT IS THE PURPOSE OF BAPTISM?*

Answers to the following questions can be found in the section above.

STUDY QUESTIONS

1. In the Patriarchal period, _____ was used to cleanse the Earth and to save Noah and his family from destruction.

2. According to 1 Peter 3:20-21, the apostle Peter referenced the Noahic flood that cleansed the Earth and said the following: "…in the days of Noah, while the ark was being prepared, in which a few, that is eight souls, were _____ through water. There is also an antitype which now saves us—_____.

3. Under the Mosaic Age, an animal's _____ was used as a symbol of purification and redemption.

4. In the Mosaic Age, _____ was used as a symbol of purification for such things as the cleansing of the priests who came to serve in the temple, and in the cleansing of lepers.

5. According to 1 Peter 1:18-19 and Romans 3:23-26, under the Christian Age, Jesus shed His precious _____ for the purpose of purification and cleansing.

6. According to Romans 3:23-26, sinners can be "_____ freely by His grace through the redemption that is in Christ Jesus, whom God set forth as a propitiation by His blood."

7. The word "justified," as used in the New Testament, carries with it the meaning of "_____ _____" or "acquitted."

8. Just as God in the Old Testament used both blood and water in purifying and cleansing, He likewise uses today under the New Covenant both

_____ and _____ to _____ the sinner.

9. According to James 2:24, people *cannot* be saved by "_____ _____."

10. According to Matthew 7:21, Jesus said, "Not everyone who says 'Lord, Lord,' shall enter the kingdom of heaven, but he who _____ the will of My Father in heaven."

11. According to Romans 6:17-18, the Bible teaches: "But God be thanked that though you were slaves of sin, yet you _____ from the heart that form of doctrine to which you were delivered. And having been set free from sin, you became slaves of righteousness."

12. According to the verse below, what is God's power to salvation? _____ _____ _____

_____

> For I am not ashamed of the gospel of Christ, for it is the power of God to salvation for everyone who believes, for the Jew first and also for the Greek (Romans 1:16).

13. According to 1 Corinthians 15:1-4, did the Gospel preached by Paul and delivered to the Corinthians include preaching about the death, burial, and resurrection of Christ? YES / NO

14. According to 2 Thessalonians 1:7-8, the Lord Jesus and his mighty angels will take vengeance on those who do not know _____, and on those who do not _____ _____ _____.

15. According to Romans 6:17 and 1 Corinthians 15:1-4, do sinners have to *literally* die, *literally* be buried, and *literally* be resurrected in order to be obedient to the Gospel? YES / NO

16. According to Romans 6:3, sinners who want to be saved must be _____ into Christ's death.

17. According to the verse below, baptism is for the _____ of sins.

> *Then Peter said to them, "Repent, and let every one of you be baptized in the name of Jesus Christ for the remission of sins; and you shall receive the gift of the Holy Spirit" (Acts 2:38).*

18. According to John 3:3, 5, Jesus told Nicodemus that in order to enter the kingdom of God, a person has to be "born of _____ and the Spirit."

19. According to the verse below, _____ washes away sin.

> *And now why are you waiting? Arise and be baptized, and wash away your sins, calling on the name of the Lord (Acts 22:16).*

20. In 1 Peter 3:21, Peter referred to baptism as that "which now _____ us."

21. According to the verses below, are all spiritual blessings (including salvation) found in Christ? YES / NO

> *Blessed be the God and Father of our Lord Jesus Christ, who has blessed us with every spiritual blessing in the heavenly places in Christ (Ephesians 1:3).*

> *Therefore I endure all things for the sake of the elect, that they also may obtain the salvation which is in Christ Jesus with eternal glory (2 Timothy 2:10).*

22. According to the verse below, a sinner gets into Christ by being _____ into Christ.

> *For as many of you as were baptized into Christ have put on Christ (Galatians 3:27).*

23. According to 1 Corinthians 12:13, baptism places a sinner into the _____ of Christ (that is to say, the church of Christ).

An ANSWER KEY for the STUDY QUESTIONS is provided in the back of the book.

DECISION POINTS

A. Have you been baptized by immersion in order to have your sins forgiven? YES / NO

B. If you were taught you were saved *before* baptism, could you have been baptized for the remission of sins (to be saved)? YES / NO

C. If you were not baptized the way God said to be baptized (by immersion) and for the right reason (for the remission of sins) could you be wrong? YES / NO

D. Do you want to go to heaven? YES / NO

E. Are you ready to be baptized for the remission of sins into the body of Christ? YES / NO

TALKING POINTS

A. According to Romans 6:3-5 and the verse below, how does a sinner come into contact with the saving blood of Christ?

    And from Jesus Christ, the faithful witness, the firstborn from the dead, and the ruler over the kings of the earth. To Him who loved us and washed us from our sins in His own blood (Revelation 1:5).

B. According to John 3:3, 5, baptism places a sinner into "something." What is that something?

C. How do the facts of Jesus' death, burial, and resurrection coincide with and form the basis of a sinner's transformation into becoming a Christian? In the other words, what is the interrelationship between the death, burial, and resurrection of Christ and the commandment for sinners to be baptized for the remission of sins?

WHO SHOULD BE BAPTIZED?

Who should be baptized? In other words, what does a person need to know or do before baptism? And what about babies? Should they be baptized? In answering these questions, let us begin by hearing the words of Jesus:

> *Go therefore and make disciples of all the nations, baptizing them in the name of the Father and of the Son and of the Holy Spirit (Matthew 28:19).*

> *...Go into all the world and preach the gospel to every creature. He who believes and is baptized will be saved... (Mark 16:15-16).*

From both of these statements, we learn that something very important must occur before one can be scripturally baptized. What is that "something"? Quite simply, it is preaching and believing. In order for a person to come to God, he or she must first *hear* (or be taught) the word of God.

> *It is written in the prophets, "And they shall all be taught by God." Therefore everyone who has heard and learned from the Father comes to Me (John 6:45).*

In addition to being *taught*, the one who wishes to be baptized must *believe* what is taught. When Jesus said, "He who believes and is baptized shall be saved," we must ask "What is it, exactly, that one must believe?" Notice again that Jesus said, "Go into all the world and preach the Gospel. He who believes (that is, he who believes the Gospel) and is baptized shall be saved." Those who desire to be baptized must believe the Gospel.

Believing the Gospel demands that we believe that Jesus is the Son of God and Savior of the world.

> *For God so loved the world that He gave His only begotten Son, that whoever believes in Him should not perish but have everlasting life (John 3:16).*

Believing in Jesus comes when we hear the word of God:

> *...faith comes by hearing, and hearing by the word of God (Romans 10:17).*

But let us notice that believing the Gospel also demands that we believe in what Jesus taught in His New Covenant. This covenant (or testament) reveals that before a person can come to God in baptism, he or she must *repent*:

> *...Repent, and let every one of you be baptized in the name of Jesus Christ for the remission of sins; and you shall receive the gift of the Holy Spirit (Acts 2:38).*

Repentance is not merely feeling sorry about our sins. Instead, the Bible teaches us that godly sorrow *leads* to repentance:

> *Now I rejoice, not that you were made sorry, but that your sorrow led to repentance. For you were made sorry in a godly manner, that you might suffer loss from us in nothing. For godly sorrow produces repentance leading to salvation, not to be regretted; but the sorrow of the world produces death (2 Corinthians 7:9-10).*

About Baptism

What, then, is repentance? To repent means to change—to change from living a life of sin to living a life of righteousness. Repentance also demands that we stop living according to our own will, and start living a life that follows in the steps of Jesus:

> *...If anyone desires to come after Me, let him deny himself, and take up his cross daily, and follow Me (Luke 9:23).*

Who, then, should be baptized? It is the person who believes the Gospel and repents of sin.

But still further, those who can be baptized are those who have *confessed.*

> *Therefore whoever confesses Me before men, him I will also confess before My Father who is in heaven (Matthew 10:32).*

Now let us put this all together: Baptism must be preceded by teaching—and then belief, repentance, and confession. So, who should be baptized? It is the sinner who is outside of Christ, who is taught, who believes, who repents, and who confesses.

But what, then, should we do about baptizing babies? Is it right or necessary to baptize a baby? Ask yourself, "Can a baby believe, repent, or confess?" No. We know that a baby does not possess the mental capacity to do these things. A baby therefore cannot obey God's command to be baptized.

It is not necessary to baptize a baby, nor is it scriptural. Baptism is for those who can hear the word of God, understand it, believe it, and, based on that understanding, obey it. Jesus said, "He who believes and is baptized will be saved" (Mark 16:16). In addition, babies are not lost. They are "safe," as Jesus said in Matthew 18:3, "Assuredly, I say to you, unless you are converted and become as little children, you will by no means enter the kingdom of heaven." We are to have the characteristics of little children, who are in the kingdom of God. Babies are not lost, and do not need to be baptized. They would not understand it. Baptism is for those who are accountable and mature, and who have the ability to act, based on their own choice.

Bobby Liddell
Bible Instructor and Minister

The only reason a baby would need to be baptized would be if the baby had sins that needed to be remitted. But according to Ezekiel 18:20, "The son shall not bear the guilt of the father, nor the father bear the guilt of the son." Deuteronomy 24:16 sets forth the principle that every man shall be put to death *for his own sins.* A baby has not transgressed the law of God (1 John 3:4). Thus, a baby does not *need* to be baptized because he has not sinned, and he does not *qualify* for baptism because he has not believed.

B. J. Clarke
Minister

Sin is something committed, not inherited. Babies and young children, therefore, do not need to be baptized.

SECTION REVIEW: *WHO SHOULD BE BAPTIZED?*

Answers to the following questions can be found in the section above.

STUDY QUESTIONS

1. According to Mark 16:16, a person must both _____ and be _____ to be saved.

2. According to John 6:45, must a person hear and learn before coming to the Father? YES / NO

3. According to John 3:16, in order to have everlasting life a person must believe (have faith) that Jesus is the only begotten _____ (of God).

4. According to Romans 10:17, faith comes by _____ God's word.

5. According to Acts 2:38, a sinner must both _____ of his or her sins and be baptized in order to be saved.

6. According to 2 Corinthians 7:9-10, is repentance "just feeling sorry" for our sins? YES / NO

7. To repent means to change—to change from living a life of _____ to living a life of righteousness.

8. According to Matthew 10:32, in order to be saved a sinner must _____.

9. According to Acts 2:38 and the verses below, does the bible teach that in order to be saved, a sinner *must* be baptized? YES / NO

    And now why are you waiting? Arise and be baptized, and wash away your sins, calling on the name of the Lord (Acts 22:16).

    There is also an antitype which now saves us—baptism (not the removal of the filth of the flesh, but the answer of a good conscience toward God), through the resurrection of Jesus Christ (1 Peter 3:21).

10. According to the verse below, can sin be inherited, or are children born in sin? YES / NO

    The soul who sins shall die. The son shall not bear the guilt of the father, nor the father bear the guilt of the son. The righteousness of the righteous shall be upon himself, and the wickedness of the wicked shall be upon himself (Ezekiel 18:20).

11. Can babies or infants believe in Christ as God's Son, repent of past sins, and confess Christ's name? YES / NO

12. According to New Testament teaching, is it scriptural to baptize babies or infants? YES / NO

An ANSWER KEY for the STUDY QUESTIONS is provided in the back of the book.

DECISION POINTS

A. If you were "baptized" as a baby, is that "baptism" scriptural? YES / NO

B. If you were "baptized" as a baby, what should you do about it?

C. Should sinners (not yet baptized) be baptized? YES / NO

D. Are you a sinner? YES / NO

E. Do you believe that the blood of Jesus can save you? YES / NO

TALKING POINTS

A. The only reason a baby or infant would need to be baptized is if the baby had sins that needed to be forgiven. According to the Bible, do babies "sin?" Why or why not?

B. Are babies scriptural candidates for baptism? Why or why not?

About Baptism

HAVE *YOU* BEEN SCRIPTURALLY BAPTIZED?

Now, let us address our last major question. As we do, let us make it very personal by talking about *you,* God, and baptism: "Have *you* been *scripturally* baptized?"

Deciding whether or not to be baptized is a very important decision. In fact, it is the most important decision a person can make. If you have never been baptized, then according to the Bible you are yet in your sins because the benefits of the Lord's saving blood can be realized only in the God-ordained act of baptism. If you have never been baptized, then according to the Bible you are not saved, and you are not in the kingdom of God:

> Jesus answered, *"Most assuredly, I say to you, unless one is born of water and the Spirit, he cannot enter the kingdom of God" (John 3:5).*
>
> *...Go into all the world and preach the gospel to every creature. He who believes and is baptized will be saved... (Mark 16:15-16).*

At the beginning of this lesson, you were asked to answer several questions, the first of which was the question about whether or not you are saved. *Are* you saved? Are you in a right relationship with God? Have you done things that you knew were wrong? Are you burdened with guilt? Has sin become a burden you can no longer bear? Are you, in fact, a sinner lost and separated from God? Or, are you perhaps uncertain about your relationship with God? Wouldn't you like to be certain? Wouldn't you like to be sure, and *know* that you are saved?

If you *are* separated from God, please know that the precious blood of Christ can justify sinners (Romans 5:9). It can cleanse your conscience (Hebrews 10:22). It can remove your sin (Revelation 1:5). It can bring sweet redemption to your heart that has been held captive by Satan (Ephesians 1:7).

However, in order to obtain forgiveness from God, you must render obedience to His will by being baptized. In fact, we would encourage and implore you to go do that this very hour. Contact the individual or church who gave you this material on *Searching for Truth,* and have someone baptize you into Christ for the remission of your sins. When you are baptized, you then can come to know the peace that passes all understanding (Philippians 4:7). You can know that you are in the family of God, the church.

When you obey the truth by being baptized for the remission of your sins, you can know that your soul is purified (1 Peter 1:22). According to Colossians 1:22-23, if you continue in the faith—being grounded and settled in the Gospel of Christ—when it comes time to leave this life, you can anticipate the mercy of God and expect Jesus to present you before the heavenly throne as one who is blameless and beyond reproach.

This decision is the most important decision of your life. But equally important—if you believe you are saved already—is the decision about whether or not what you did to become saved is consistent with the will of God. Did you obey the commandments of God, or the commandments of men? Do your answers to the questions at the beginning of this lesson match those revealed in God's word?

For example, were you taught that, in order to become a Christian, you simply needed to believe in Jesus by asking Him to come into your heart? Were you taught that to be saved, you had to recite a prewritten prayer? Or did you become a Christian by believing on Jesus, confessing His name, repenting of your sins, and being baptized?

If you were baptized, were you baptized by sprinkling, pouring, or immersion? Were you baptized as an infant or as an adult? True baptism as prescribed by God is by immersion, and requires both faith and repentance. As we have seen, baptism is for the purpose of uniting a sinner with the death of Christ to wash away sin. Was this the reason *you* were baptized? Were you baptized to be saved? Or were you baptized believing that you *already* had been saved? According to the Bible, baptism is for the remission of sins. So if you were taught that you were saved *before* baptism, could you have been baptized for the remission of sins?

If your answers have not matched the truths we have presented from the Bible, we encourage you to correct your situation immediately. Being baptized for the right reason, in the right way, and according to the truth of the Gospel, is absolutely critical.

This is exactly what happened when, in the city of Ephesus, the apostle Paul found some disciples who had not been baptized for the right reason. This story is recorded in the nineteenth chapter of Acts, and reveals that there were some who were practicing a *form* of Christianity (and who had even been baptized). However, after further inquiry by Paul, he soon discovered that their baptism had not been done according to the will of God. It was at that point that Paul corrected their false ideas about their baptism. They responded by being baptized again. This time, however, their baptism was done in the name of Christ Jesus. Their first baptism was no doubt done with the best of intentions, but it was not according to the truth of the Gospel.

How many today have been baptized with the best of intentions, yet their baptism was not done according to truth? If your baptism, for example, was not done by immersion, or for the remission of sins, can you honestly say that you were baptized according to the divine pattern revealed in the word of God?

Remember, you will be judged by the word of God. Can you say—without any doubt—that your baptism was done *exactly* as the Bible prescribes?

Once more, that pattern requires that a sinner follow the steps of salvation, which involve…

- Hearing the Gospel (John 6:45; Romans 10:17)
- Believing the Gospel (Mark 16:16; John 8:24)
- Repenting of sins (Luke 13:3)
- Confessing that Jesus is the Son of God (Matthew 10:32-33; Romans 10:10; Acts 8:37)
- Being immersed (baptized) for the remission of sins (Acts 2:38, 22:16; 1 Peter 3:21)
- Living faithfully until death (Revelation 2:10).

If you are not *absolutely certain* whether or not you have followed the steps completely, then please do not take a chance on missing heaven. Please obey the truth today. Remember that the truth and *only the truth* is what will make you free (John 8:32).

SECTION REVIEW: *HAVE YOU BEEN SCRIPTURALLY BAPTIZED?*

Answers to the following questions can be found in the section above.

STUDY QUESTIONS

1. According to Mark 16:15-16, Jesus said, "Go into all the world and preach the gospel to _____ creature. He who believes and is _____ will be saved."

2. The precious blood of Christ can _____ sinners, cleanse your _____, remove sin, and bring sweet _____.

3. When you are baptized, you can come to know the peace that passes all understanding. You can know that you are in the _____ of _____, the church.

4. According to the verse below, when you obey the truth by being baptized for the remission of sins, you can know that your soul is _____.

   Since you have purified your souls in obeying the truth through the Spirit in sincere love of the brethren, love one another fervently with a pure heart (1 Peter 1:22).

5. According to the verses below, if a person has been baptized *incorrectly,* must they be baptized *correctly?* YES / NO

   And it happened, while Apollos was at Corinth, that Paul, having passed through the upper regions, came to Ephesus. And finding some disciples he said to them, "Did you receive the Holy Spirit when you believed?" So they said to him, "We have not so much as heard whether there is a Holy Spirit." And he said to them, "Into what then were you baptized?" So they said, "Into John's baptism." Then Paul said, "John indeed baptized with a baptism of repentance, saying to the people that they should believe on Him who would come after him, that is, on Christ Jesus." When they heard this, they were baptized in the name of the Lord Jesus (Acts 19:1-5).

6. The New Testament pattern that a sinner must follow to be saved involves the following (see page 99):

   a. _____ the Gospel (see verse below).

   So then faith comes by hearing, and hearing by the word of God (Romans 10:17).

   b. _____ the Gospel (Mark 16:16).

   c. _____ of sins (see verse below).

   Truly, these times of ignorance God overlooked, but now commands all men everywhere to repent (Acts 17:30).

    d. _____ that Jesus is the Son of God (see verse below).

       Therefore whoever confesses Me before men, him I will also confess before My Father who is in heaven (Matthew 10:32).

    e. Being _____ for the remission of sins (see verse below).

       And now why are you waiting? Arise and be baptized, and wash away your sins, calling on the name of the Lord (Acts 22:16).

    f. Living _____ until death (see verse below).

       Do not fear any of those things which you are about to suffer. Indeed, the devil is about to throw some of you into prison, that you may be tested, and you will have tribulation ten days. Be faithful until death, and I will give you the crown of life (Revelation 2:10).

7. According to the verses below, only the truth as found in the words of Jesus can make us _____.

       Then Jesus said to those Jews who believed Him, "If you abide in My word, you are My disciples indeed. And you shall know the truth, and the truth shall make you free" (John 8:31-32).

An ANSWER KEY for the STUDY QUESTIONS is provided in the back of the book.

DECISION POINTS

At the beginning of the chapter on *Searching for Truth about Baptism,* you were asked to answer several important questions about salvation. Go back and look at your answers and compare them with what you have learned in this lesson, and then answer the following questions:

A. Are you now in a saved relationship with God? YES / NO

B. Do you believe that Jesus Christ is the Son of God? YES / NO

C. As we have seen, Jesus commands repentance. Are you ready to start making the changes in your life that Jesus commands and to live for God? YES / NO

D. According to the New Testament, if you have not been baptized for the remission of sins in the name of Jesus Christ, are you saved? YES / NO

E. According to the New Testament, if you have not been baptized in the proper manner, and for the right reason, are you saved? YES / NO

F. According to the verse below, do you love Jesus? YES / NO

       If you love Me, keep My commandments (John 14:15).

G. Do you want to obey Jesus? YES / NO

H. When do you want to obey Jesus? _____

I. Since Jesus wants you to be baptized, and now that you understand the necessity of being baptized right now, wouldn't it please Jesus for you to be baptized right now? YES / NO

J. Will you begin today to renounce all other religious names and identify yourself as a Christian only? YES / NO

K. Consider the verse below. After your baptism, will you be faithful in attending the services of the Lord's church? YES / NO

       And let us consider one another in order to stir up love and good works, not forsaking the assembling of ourselves together, as is the manner of some, but exhorting one another, and so much the more as you see the Day approaching (Hebrews 10:24-25).

Chapter 6

TALKING POINTS

A. Is it enough to have "good intentions" when one is baptized?

B. What is the single most important decision a person can ever make in his or her life?

C. Do all religious groups teach that baptism is essential for salvation? Why or why not?

D. What false doctrines or traditions of men are in existence, which overlook the essentially of water baptism? How does scripture refute these false ideas?

CONCLUSION

Friend, have you obeyed *the truth,* or did you obey the commandments of men? The apostle Peter reminded his readers that when they obeyed the truth, their souls were purified. If you obeyed the commandments or traditions of men in wanting to become a Christian, then you did not *obey truth.*

> *Since you have purified your souls in obeying the truth through the Spirit in sincere love of the brethren, love one another fervently with a pure heart (1 Peter 1:22).*

Purified souls come from obeying the pure truth. The truth that comes from Jesus, as revealed in Matthew 7:21-23, is that not everyone who calls upon the name of the Lord will be saved. Instead, those who "do the will of the Father" will be saved.

Have *you* done the will of the Father? Have you been baptized for the remission of your sins in the name of the Father, Son, and Holy Spirit (Matthew 28:19) in order to become a member of the church of Jesus Christ? If not, do not delay another minute. Go in search of the church of Christ, and ask one of its members to baptize you for the remission of your sins. After your baptism, begin worshiping according to the truth of the Gospel. Call yourself a Christian—and nothing more. Give your life completely to the Lord and His church. Seek first the kingdom of God, and never forsake the opportunity to assemble with the church. And finally, always remember these words from Jesus:

> *Then Jesus said to those Jews who believed in Him, "If you abide in My word, you are My disciples indeed. And you shall know the truth, and the truth shall make you free" (John 8:31-32).*

Now is the right time. *Now* is the day of salvation. *Now* is the time to believe and obey the truth. Now that you know the truth, will you this very hour obey it? Tomorrow may be too late. Jesus said, *"If you love me, keep My commandments"* (John 14:15). If you truly love Jesus, then you will want to respond to the truth about the Creator, to the truth about authority in religion, to the truth about the church, to the truth about the house of God, and to the truth about baptism.

How will you respond? Will you believe and obey the truth? Your eternal destiny will be determined by what you do with the truth. It is now in your hands. We hope and pray that you will live according to the truth.

CHAPTER REVIEW
Answers to the following questions can be found within this chapter.

STUDY QUESTIONS

1. In the New Testament, _____ was a very important part of God's plan in saving souls.

2. Is sprinkling or pouring water on someone as a form of baptism a part of authentic Christianity? YES / NO

3. According to Romans 6:17-18, sinners who were slaves to sin did not obey the doctrine (teaching) about the death, burial, and resurrection of Christ, but instead they obeyed a _____ of the doctrine to become servants of righteousness.

4. _____ is for the remission of sins, and also the means by which one becomes a servant of righteousness, a child

About Baptism

of God, and a _____.

5. Should small children or babies be baptized? YES / NO

6. According to Mark 16:16 and Acts 2:38, what must a person do

    before baptism? _____ and _____.

7. According to Luke 9:23, Jesus said, "If anyone desires to come

    after me, let him _____ himself, and take up his

    cross daily, and _____ me."

FOCUS QUESTIONS

1. According to John 8:31-32, Jesus said, "If you abide in my

    _____ then are you my _____

    indeed. And you shall know the _____, and the

    _____ shall make you free."

2. According to John 3:20-21, Jesus said that "he who

    _____ _____

    _____ comes to the light."

3. According to Revelation 2:10 and Colossians 1:22-23, a person

    must be faithful even "until _____" in order to
    eventually live in heaven.

An ANSWER KEY for the STUDY QUESTIONS and FOCUS QUES-
TIONS is provided in the back of the book.

THINGS YOU SHOULD KNOW

- In both the Old and New Testaments, God used the elements of water and blood in the process of sanctifying and cleansing the sinner.
- The new birth requires baptism by immersion.
- Baptism is essential for salvation.
- The act of baptism is synonymous with obeying the Gospel.
- Those who do not obey the Gospel will suffer eternal damnation.
- Sin is not inherited, but a deliberate act of the will.

- Babies are not born in sin and therefore do not need to be baptized—they are safe.
- To be scripturally baptized one must hear the Gospel, believe, repent, and confess.
- Baptism for the remission of sins places a sinner into the body of Christ.
- Those who are a part of the body of Christ are known as Christians.
- To remain as a true Christian one must continue in the words of Christ.

DIGGING DEEPER

The material below is intended for those people who would like to study this subject further. It contains information that was not necessarily discussed in the lesson.

 ### THE IMPORTANCE OF OBEDIENCE TO GOD'S MESSAGE

No more shall every man teach his neighbor, and every man his brother, saying, "Know the LORD," for they all shall know Me, from the least of them to the greatest of them, says the LORD. For I will forgive their iniquity, and their sin I will remember no more (Jeremiah 31:34).

He who rejects Me, and does not receive My words, has that which judges him—the word that I have spoken will judge him in the last day (John 12:48).

If you love Me, keep My commandments (John 14:15).

You are My friends if you do whatever I command you (John 15:14).

For the message of the cross is foolishness to those who are perishing, but to us who are being saved it is the power of God. For it is written: "I will destroy the wisdom of the wise, and bring to nothing the understanding of the prudent." Where is the wise? Where is the scribe? Where is the disputer of this age? Has not God made foolish the wisdom of this world? For since, in the wisdom of God, the world through wisdom did not know God, it pleased God through the foolishness of the message preached to save those who believe (1 Corinthians 1:18-21).

THINGS TO THINK ABOUT…WHEN DIGGING DEEPER

1. According to Jeremiah 31:34, is one of the blessings of obeying God having our sins forgiven? YES / NO

2. According to 1 Corinthians 1:18-21, do some people view God's message as "foolish?" YES / NO

3. According to John 12:48, *is* God's message foolish? YES / NO

4. Did Jesus say in John 14:15 and John 15:14 that if we love Him, we will obey Him? YES / NO

THE IMPORTANCE OF CHRIST'S BLOOD

For this is My blood of the new covenant, which is shed for many for the remission of sins (Matthew 26:28).

Being justified freely by His grace through the redemption that is in Christ Jesus, whom God set forth as *a propitiation by His blood, through faith, to demonstrate His righteousness, because in His forbearance God had passed over the sins that were previously committed, to demonstrate at the present time His righteousness, that He might be just and the justifier of the one who has faith in Jesus (Romans 3:24-26).*

Or do you not know that as many of us as were baptized into Christ Jesus were baptized into His death? Therefore we were buried with Him through baptism into death, that just as Christ was raised from the dead by the glory of the Father, even so we also should walk in newness of life. For if we have been united together in the likeness of His death, certainly we also shall be in the likeness *of* His *resurrection (Romans 6:3-5).*

In Him we have redemption through His blood, the forgiveness of sins, according to the riches of His grace (Ephesians 1:7).

Not with the blood of goats and calves, but with His own blood He entered the Most Holy Place once for all, having obtained eternal redemption. For if the blood of bulls and goats and the ashes of a heifer, sprinkling the unclean, sanctifies for the purifying of the flesh, how much more shall the blood of Christ, who through the eternal Spirit offered Himself without spot to God, cleanse your conscience from dead works to serve the living God? (Hebrews 9:12-14).

And they sang a new song, saying: "You are worthy to take the scroll, And to open its seals; For You were slain, And have redeemed us to God by Your blood Out of every tribe and tongue and people and nation" (Revelation 5:9).

THINGS TO THINK ABOUT…WHEN DIGGING DEEPER

5. Do Matthew 26:28 and Ephesians 1:7 teach that Christ shed His blood so that we could have remission (forgiveness) of sins? YES / NO

6. Does Romans 3:24-26 teach that in order for us to have forgiveness of sins through the blood of Christ, we must have faith in Christ (that is, we must obey Him) ? YES / NO

7. The soul saving blood of Jesus was shed in His death. Does Romans 6:3-5 teach that baptism puts us into Jesus' death, the very place where that blood was shed? YES / NO

8. Does Hebrews 9:12-14 teach that we can be cleansed by the blood of bulls and goats? YES / NO

9. Does Revelation 5:9 teach that Christ redeemed us by His blood? YES / NO

THE IMPORTANCE OF BAPTISM

Now when they heard this, *they were cut to the heart, and said to Peter and the rest of the apostles, "Men* and *brethren, what shall we do?" Then Peter said to them, "Repent, and let every one of you be baptized in the name of Jesus Christ for the remission of sins; and you shall receive the gift of the Holy Spirit" (Acts 2:37-38).*

And he brought them out and said, "Sirs, what must I do to be saved?" So they said, "Believe on the Lord Jesus Christ, and you will be saved, you and your household." Then they spoke the word of the Lord to him and to all who were in his house. And he took them the same hour of the night and washed their stripes. And immediately he and all his family were baptized (Acts 16:30-33).

And now why are you waiting? Arise and be baptized, and wash away your sins, calling on the name of the Lord (Acts 22:16).

For as many of you as were baptized into Christ have put on Christ (Galatians 3:27).

There is *one body and one Spirit, just as you were called in one hope of your calling; one Lord, one faith, one baptism (Ephesians 4:4-5).*

Husbands, love your wives, just as Christ also loved the church and gave Himself for her, that He might sanctify and cleanse her with the washing of water by the word (Ephesians 5:25-26).

About Baptism

In Him you were also circumcised with the circumcision made without hands, by putting off the body of the sins of the flesh, by the circumcision of Christ, buried with Him in baptism, in which you also were raised with Him *through faith in the working of God, who raised Him from the dead (Colossians 2:11-12).*

But when the kindness and the love of God our Savior toward man appeared, not by works of righteousness which we have done, but according to His mercy He saved us, through the washing of regeneration and renewing of the Holy Spirit, whom He poured out on us abundantly through Jesus Christ our Savior, that having been justified by His grace we should become heirs according to the hope of eternal life (Titus 3:4-7).

There is also an antitype which now saves us—baptism (not the removal of the filth of the flesh, but the answer of a good conscience toward God), through the resurrection of Jesus Christ (1 Peter 3:21).

THINGS TO THINK ABOUT…WHEN DIGGING DEEPER

10. When Peter's audience asked what they should do in Acts 2:37, Peter responded in the next verse that they should

    _____ and be _____ .

11. In Acts 16:30, the Philippian jailer asked, "Sirs, what must I do to be saved?" In Acts 16:33, he and all his family were

    _____ immediately.

12. According to Galatians 3:27, when we are baptized

    _____ Christ, we have _____

    _____ Christ.

13. According to Paul's comment in Ephesians 4:5, how many

    baptisms exist today? _____

14. In Ephesians 5:25-26, the phrase "with the washing of water"

    refers to what action? _____

15. According to Colossians 2:12, when we are baptized, we are "buried with Christ in baptism." Can we be "buried" in a "pouring" or "sprinkling" ritual that is substituted for full-body immersion? YES / NO

16. According to Titus 3:4-5, God "saved us through the washing of regeneration." The phrase "through the washing of regeneration" refers to what action? _____

17. What did Peter say "now saves us" (1 Peter 3:21)?

    _____

 ## THE IMPORTANCE OF "WORKS OF GOD" (AS OPPOSED TO "WORKS OF RIGHTEOUSNESS" DEVISED BY MEN)

Then God saw their works, that they turned from their evil way; and God relented from the disaster that He had said He would bring upon them, and He did not do it (Jonah 3:10).

For everyone practicing evil hates the light and does not come to the light, lest his deeds should be exposed. But he who does the truth comes to the light, that his deeds may be clearly seen, that they have been done in God (John 3:20-21).

Therefore by the deeds of the law no flesh will be justified in His sight, for by the law is the knowledge of sin (Romans 3:20).

Knowing that a man is not justified by the works of the law but by faith in Jesus Christ, even we have believed in Christ Jesus, that we might be justified by faith in Christ and not by the works of the law; for by the works of the law no flesh shall be justified (Galatians 2:16).

For by grace you have been saved through faith, and that not of yourselves; it is the gift of God, not of works, lest anyone should boast. For we are His workmanship, created in Christ Jesus for good works, which God prepared beforehand that we should walk in them (Ephesians 2:8-10).

But when the kindness and the love of God our Savior toward man appeared, not by works of righteousness which we have done, but according to His mercy He saved us, through the washing of regeneration and renewing of the Holy Spirit, whom He poured out on us abundantly through Jesus Christ our Savior, that having been justified by His grace we should become heirs according to the hope of eternal life (Titus 3:4-7).

You see then that a man is justified by works, and not by faith only (James 2:24).

THINGS TO THINK ABOUT…WHEN DIGGING DEEPER

18. Does Jonah 3:10 teach that God *does* see our good works, and that those good works *do* influence His decisions about us? YES / NO

19. Does John 3:20-21 teach that "our deeds may be clearly seen, that they have been done in God?" YES / NO

20. According to Romans 3:20, can we save ourselves through doing "deeds of the law?" YES / NO

21. Does Galatians 2:16 say that we are saved "by works of the law?" YES / NO

22. Does Ephesians 2:9 teach that we are saved by works? YES / NO

23. Does Ephesians 2:10 teach that there are works that God requires us to walk in (do)? YES / NO

24. Does Titus 3:4-5 teach that we are saved "by works of righteousness which we have done?" YES / NO

25. Does James 2:24 teach that "a man is justified by works, and not by faith only?" YES / NO

26. If the Bible teaches that works *do not* save us, yet it also teaches that works *do* save us, does that show us that there are *two different types of works* under consideration? YES / NO

27. Is it true to say that one type of works—"works of righteousness which we have done"—*cannot* save us? YES / NO

28. Is it true to say that one type of works—"works of God" (that is, the works that God has commanded us to do)—*can* save us? YES / NO

 THE BLESSINGS OF BEING BAPTIZED

And with many other words he testified and exhorted them, saying, "Be saved from this perverse generation." Then those who gladly received his word were baptized; and that day about three thousand souls were added to them. … praising God and having favor with all the people. And the Lord added to the church daily those who were being saved (Acts 2:40-41,47).

Or do you not know that as many of us as were baptized into Christ Jesus were baptized into His death? Therefore we were buried with Him through baptism into death, that just as Christ was raised from the dead by the glory of the Father, even so we also should walk in newness of life (Romans 6:3-4).

Blessed be the God and Father of our Lord Jesus Christ, who has blessed us with every spiritual blessing in the heavenly places in Christ (Ephesians 1:3).

Therefore I endure all things for the sake of the elect, that they also may obtain the salvation which is in Christ Jesus with eternal glory (2 Timothy 2:10).

THINGS TO THINK ABOUT…WHEN DIGGING DEEPER

29. Does Acts 2:40-41,47 teach that God adds those who have been baptized to "the saved" (the church)? YES / NO

30. According to Ephesians 1:3, where are "all spiritual blessings" found? _____ _____

31. According to 2 Timothy 2:10, where is salvation found? _____ _____ _____

32. If a person is not in Christ, can they have any spiritual blessings or salvation?

33. According to Romans 6:3-4, what action puts a person "into Christ?" _____

34. Consider carefully: Have you been baptized in the way the Bible teaches to be put into Christ and have access to spiritual blessings and salvation? If not, why not?

An ANSWER KEY for the DIGGING DEEPER QUESTIONS is provided in the back of the book.

Chapter 1 – Searching for Truth
ABOUT THE TRUTH

1. 153,000
2. MANY
3. a. NO; b. YES; c. the will of My Father
4. YES
5. truth
6. unrighteous behavior, false religious practices, traditions
7. a. Jesus; b. NO
8. YES
9. YES
10. truth
11. wrong
12. NO

Chapter 2 - Searching for Truth
ABOUT THE CREATOR

WHAT CAN NATURE TELL US ABOUT GOD?
1. nature
2. excuse
3. intelligent Designer
4. masterful Architect
5. tree, nature
6. NO
7. NO
8. NO

HOW CAN WE KNOW THE MIND OF GOD?
1. NO
2. NO
3. scripture
4. YES
5. Bible
6. God breathed
7. Holy Spirit
8. NO

WHAT DOES THE BIBLE TELL US ABOUT GOD?
1. good news
2. YES
3. NO
4. repent
5. far
6. love
7. repent
8. YES
9. NO
10. YES
11. NO
12. YES

CHAPTER 2 REVIEW
Study Questions
1. YES
2. God
3. judgment
4. YES

Focus Questions
1. NO
2. NO
3. YES

DIGGING DEEPER…
1. YES
2. YES
3. God
4. world, everything
5. all things
6. YES
7. YES
8. heart
9. all things
10. account
11. everything
12. spoke, commanded
13. all things

14. NO
15. Almighty
16. cannot contain
17. flee
18. YES
19. NO
20. NO
21. compassions
22. YES
23. good gift, perfect gift
24. YES
25. love

Chapter 3 – Searching For Truth
ABOUT AUTHORITY IN RELIGION

WHAT IS AUTHORITY?
1. where to find them
2. YES
3. command, decision
4. YES
5. NO
6. YES

WHO, OR WHAT, IS THE AUTHORITY IN RELIGION?
1. YES
2. YES
3. YES
4. YES
5. the Father (God)
6. church

HOW IS THIS AUTHORITY MADE KNOWN?
1. NO
2. His Son
3. YES
4. YES
5. written
6. Holy Spirit
7. law, Christ

8. rulebook
9. YES
10. Christ (Jesus)
11. YES
12. spirit, life

IS THERE MORE THAN ONE STANDARD OF AUTHORITY TODAY?
1. YES
2. YES
3. NO
4. life, godliness
5. NO
6. all
7. NO
8. accursed
9. once for all

WHAT IS THE DIFFERENCE BETWEEN THE OLD TESTAMENT AND THE NEW TESTAMENT?
1. YES
2. our learning
3. fulfill
4. new covenant
5. vanish away
6. law, force
7. tutor (schoolmaster)
8. YES
9. YES
10. YES
11. YES
12. keep the Sabbath
13. authority, written

CHAPTER 3 REVIEW
Study Questions
1. all
2. written
3. life, godliness

Focus Questions
1. NO
2. NO
3. word

DIGGING DEEPER…
1. truth
2. tongue
3. light, understanding
4. YES
5. NO

6. truth
7. YES
8. lie
9. spoke, moved
10. YES
11. NO
12. death
13. NO
14. NO
15. YES
16. searching the Scriptures daily
17. world, God
18. YES
19. God, Jesus Christ
20. wise, foolish
21. YES
22. truth
23. free
24. YES

Chapter 4 – Searching For Truth
ABOUT THE CHURCH

WHAT IS THE CHURCH?
1. called out
2. YES
3. YES
4. YES
5. YES
6. baptized, remission of sins
7. saved
8. saved
9. YES
10. house of God, church
11. YES
12. living stones
13. a. Jesus; b. Jesus; c. hear, believe, repent, confess, baptism

IS THE CHURCH ESSENTIAL AND IMPORTANT?
1. NO

2. YES
3. church, eternal purpose
4. NO
5. YES
6. kingdom (church)
7. YES
8. His body
9. YES
10. NO
11. one church
12. NO

MUST THE CHURCH BE UNIFIED?
1. NO
2. NO
3. divisions, joined together
4. YES
5. no other name
6. one
7. YES
8. YES
9. YES

CHAPTER 4 REVIEW
Study Questions
1. My
2. saved
3. NO

Focus Questions
1. NO
2. one
3. a. universal (Ephesians 5:25); b. specific (as in the assembly; Hebrews 2:12)

DIGGING DEEPER…
1. Jesus
2. Jesus
3. YES
4. the church
5. YES
6. foreordained, manifest
7. Jesus
8. rest
9. YES
10. NO
11. Christians
12. death, eternal life
13. Christ (Jesus)
14. NO
15. crown of life

Chapter 5 – Searching For Truth
ABOUT THE HOUSE OF GOD

WHO BUILT THE HOUSE OF GOD?
1. church
2. YES
3. a. Jesus; b. Jesus
4. head, all
5. all, heaven, earth
6. YES
7. NO
8. YES
9. YES

WHAT ARE THE UNIQUE CHARACTERISTICS OF THE HOUSE OF GOD?
1. forever
2. a. YES; b. NO; c. YES
3. a. elders/bishops; b. YES; c. YES; d. YES; e. NO
4. YES
5. NO
6. YES
7. a. God's word (the Bible); b. YES
8. YES
9. pray
10. spoke (preached, proclaimed)
11. give (contribute)
12. break bread
13. sing
14. NO
15. music
16. YES
17. YES

CAN WE ESTABLISH THE HOUSE OF GOD TODAY?
1. YES
2. traditions
3. obey
4. keep company

5. YES
6. add, take

CHAPTER 5 REVIEW
Study Questions
1. truth
2. temple
3. Christian

Focus Questions
1. Christ (Jesus)
2. characteristics
3. YES

DIGGING DEEPER…
1. NO
2. YES
3. the kingdom of God
4. the kingdom (the church)
5. YES
6. NO
7. Christians
8. YES
9. YES
10. saints
11. Christians
12. YES
13. YES
14. YES
15. YES
16. YES
17. YES
18. spirit, truth
19. YES
20. YES
21. in, out of
22. YES
23. continue earnestly
24. YES
25. prosper
26. cheerful giver
27. NO
28. the Lord's death
29. understanding
30. heart
31. plentiful, few
32. YES
33. death, life
34. peace, edify
35. YES
36. YES
37. greater

38. NO
39. God (the Father)
40. YES
41. to and fro
42. words
43. doctrine
44. save
45. proud, nothing
46. sound doctrine
47. integrity, reverence, incorruptibility, sound speech
48. NO
49. one
50. Christ Jesus
51. YES
52. eternal inheritance
53. Jesus Christ
54. sins

Chapter 6 – Searching For Truth
ABOUT BAPTISM

WHAT IS BAPTISM?
1. purification
2. down into
3. YES
4. YES
5. NO
6. NO
7. immerse
8. baptisteries

WHAT IS THE PURPOSE OF BAPTISM?
1. water
2. saved, baptism
3. blood
4. water
5. blood
6. justified
7. not guilty

8. blood, water, justify
9. faith only
10. does
11. obeyed
12. the gospel of Christ
13. YES
14. God, obey the gospel
15. NO
16. baptized
17. remission (forgiveness)
18. water
19. baptism
20. saves
21. YES
22. baptized
23. body

WHO SHOULD BE BAPTIZED?
1. believe, baptized
2. YES
3. Son
4. hearing
5. repent
6. NO
7. sin
8. confess
9. YES
10. NO
11. NO
12. NO

HAVE YOU BEEN SCRIPTURALLY BAPTIZED?
1. every, baptized
2. justify, heart, redemption
3. family, God (or body, Christ; or kingdom, God)
4. purified
5. YES
6. a. hearing; b. believing; c. repenting; d. confessing; e. immersed/baptized; f. faithfully
7. free

CHAPTER 6 REVIEW
Study Questions
1. water
2. NO
3. form (pattern)
4. Baptism, Christian
5. NO

6. believe, repent
7. deny, follow

Focus Questions
1. word, disciples, truth, truth
2. does the truth
3. death

DIGGING DEEPER…
1. YES
2. YES
3. NO
4. YES
5. YES
6. YES
7. YES
8. NO
9. YES
10. repent, baptized
11. baptized
12. into, put on
13. one
14. baptism
15. NO
16. baptism
17. baptism
18. YES
19. YES
20. NO
21. NO
22. NO
23. YES
24. NO
25. YES
26. YES
27. YES
28. YES
29. YES
30. in Christ
31. in Christ Jesus
32. NO
33. baptism

E-book Available

The *Searching for Truth Study Guide* is also available in e-book format. It can be downloaded for free from Google Bookstore and the Apple iBookstore, or for a minimum charge from the Amazon Kindle Store.

Online Resources from WVBS

World Video Bible School has always tried to make our material accessible to all. Most of our videos are available for free online. The following websites contain full-length videos designed to address specific topics.

SearchingForTruth.org & BuscandoLaVerdad.org
Evangelism websites presenting an introduction to the Gospel.

BeingSaved.org
Evangelism website addressing the understanding of the Gospel's plan of salvation.

WhyAreThereSoManyChurches.com
Evangelism website addressing this simple, yet often asked question.

TheTruthAbout.net
Topical website addressing important modern issues, including "Moral Issues," "Worship" and numerous other subjects.

EvilPainAndSuffering.com
Topical website addressing the "Problem of Evil" argument against God.

PregnancyDecisions.org
Topical website presenting a candid look at the choices a woman faces in an unexpected pregnancy.

AbstinenceOrSex.com
Topical website addressing the struggles teenagers and young adults encounter in a world promoting sexual activity.

WVBS.org/video
Find our latest online video resources here.

School.WVBS.org
This Online Bible School provides students with a comprehensive, in-depth study, and is designed for anyone who wants a focused, organized, study-at-your-own-pace environment to increase their Bible knowledge.

Where do we go when we die?

The World
(Place of life)

The Lost

The Saved

Sheol or Hades
(Place of the Dead)

Death

Death

Narrow Gate

Wide Gate

Great Fixed Gulf

Paradise

Torments

Resurrection

Judgment Day

Condemned

Rewarded

"Come"

"Depart"

Hell

Heaven

"Depart"
Depart..into everlasting fire (Matthew 25:41)

"Come"
Come ye blessed... inherit the kingdom (Matthew 25:34)

SAVED : The Lord added to the church daily those who were being saved (Acts 2:47)

THE LOST : Those who do not know God, and on those who do not obey the gospel of our Lord Jesus Christ (2 Thessalonians 1:7-8)

DEATH : And it is appointed for men to die once, but after this the judgment (Hebrews 9:27)

WIDE GATE : Wide is the gate and broad is the way that leads to destruction, and there are many who go in by it (Matthew 7:13)

NARROW GATE : Narrow is the gate and difficult is the way which leads to life, and there are few who find it (Matthew 7:14)

PARADISE : You will be with Me in Paradise (Luke 23:43)

TORMENTS : Being in torments in Hades (Luke 16:23)

RESURRECTION : Resurrection of the dead (1 Corinthians 15:42-44)

JUDGMENT DAY : And it is appointed for men to die once, but after this the judgment (Hebrews 9:27)

HEAVEN : An inheritance reserved in heaven for you (1 Peter 1:4)

HELL : God is able to destroy both soul and body in hell (Matthew 10:28)

GREAT GULF : Between us and you there is a great gulf fixed (Luke 16:26)